Profiles, Situations, Characters

Inspired by Theophrastus,

Jean de la Bruyère

and Álvaro Uribe

Profiles, Situations, Characters

Inspired by Theophrastus,

Jean de la Bruyère

and Álvaro Uribe

Jorge Pinto Mazal

Jorge Pinto Books, Inc.
Washington DC

JORGE
PINTO
BOOKS

Profiles, Situations, Characters.
Inspired by Theophrastus, Jean de la Bruyère
and Álvaro Uribe

Design Charles King (www.ckmm.com)
Cover image: Federico Cantú

ISBN: 979-8-9909299-9-9

Contents

Introduction

The idea of writing these notes about human nature based on the attributes of characters from my favorite novels was originally inspired by Álvaro Uribe's book *Characters*. In that text, it was possible to discover the authors Theophrastus and Jean de la Bruyère, both essayists who published important books in their time describing prototypes or characters.

My philosophical and psychological ideas are presented in a general manner and may not always be precise. The human condition is a concept frequently explored by philosophers, writers, and thinkers to describe the fundamental aspects of human existence—those universal experiences, emotions, and struggles that define what it means to be human.

As defined by Hannah Arendt, the human condition encompasses "the basic characteristics of human existence, such as birth, death, labor, and action, which shape our shared reality." Similarly, Jean-Paul Sartre emphasized that the human condition is marked by freedom and responsibility, stating; "Man is condemned to be free; because once thrown into the world, he is responsible for everything he does."

In my analysis, I draw from these perspectives while also incorporating my own interpretations and writing style. The purpose is to explore these ideas—whether through direct quotations from referenced authors or through my reflections—to better understand the shared and individual dimensions of human experience.

To add some basic analytical framework beyond the literary content of the books I cite, I selectively incorporated concepts from relevant thinkers, philosophers, historians, and psychologists for each category or character presented in the essay.

I acknowledge the intricate nature and potential contradictions inherent in the distinct character headings. As real individuals simultaneously embody multiple archetypes, literary characters in the quoted novels serve as concentrated distillations of human traits, and also exhibit this phenomenon. Consequently, the arbitrarily selected categories cannot be regarded as the exclusive characteristic even if in the novel or literature text it can be a defining one. The categories presented here frequently overlap and interact—the obsessed may also be solitary, the seducer may harbor deep insecurities. This fluidity reflects the genuine complexity of human psychology rather than representing analytical weakness. More problematically, some sections contain questionable interpretations. In certain instances, I have opted to quote or provide a partial description of a plot to elucidate the character's perspective, rather than engaging in speculative theorizing.

In the course of reading Álvaro Uribe's book, "*Characters*", I was drawn to explore the works of the Greek author Theophrastus. In the Prologue, Álvaro Uribe asserts that there would be no epic poetry without the *Iliad*, no lyric poetry without Stesichorus, no philosophical dialogue without

Plato, and, more modestly, there would be no characters without Theophrastus.

Eduardo Fernández, researcher at the Institute of Philological Research of UNAM, in the introduction to one of the latest editions of *Theophrastus*'s book, considers it unlikely that the known texts are original, since the first versions are interpretations by Byzantine authors and the first recognized versions date from the 17th century, "with Isaac Casaubon's edition, *The Characters of Theophrastus* (1592), that of Juan Cornelio de Paw, in Utrecht in 1738, and that of Ignacio López de Ayala (1782)." In the Proem, Theophrastus writes at about ninety-nine years old, after carefully observing men of good and bad habits, and "decides to describe the conduct of some and others and expose 'how they behave in their daily lives.'"

The French novelist and historian Jean de la Bruyère translated Theophrastus's aforementioned text into French in 1636 and wrote a similar work with his reflections and observations of his contemporaries, organizing them under a certain number of headings, all called "Characters." The book was published in 1688 under the original title *Les Caractères ou les Moeurs de ce siècle*. The publication of the book brought him numerous enemies, who recognized themselves or their relatives in the pages of the text. In 1691, he strove to be elected a member of the French Academy, but his efforts did not prosper until two years later with the support of his friends Racine, Boileau, and Pontchartrain, who used their influence to secure his nomination. His welcoming speech to the Academy was generally not well received; his defended the supporters of the classical and attacked the "moderns," and also included a satirical preface emulating *The Characters*, which ridiculed his enemies. The cited book is divided into sixteen chapters, among which stand out those dedicated to women, fortune, affection, the court, people of merit, humanity, fashion, opinions, and freethinkers.

The idea of finding in novels descriptions of situations and different behaviors or characteristics of humans is also inspired by the fifty types of emotions contained in the famous work, *Ethics: Demonstrated in Geometrical Order* by Baruch Spinoza, one of the most important and influential philosophers. Likewise, also useful for the conception of this essay are the references to the concept of *Needs* that, according to Schopenhauer, determine human behavior.

The text presented below does not have an academic format and does not pretend to have the rigor, character, or color of the two texts by the aforementioned authors. It is rather an arbitrary selection of texts from classic and contemporary novels whose stories are linked to situations or to the character of characters with certain characteristics or concepts.

Several sections are related to everyday human tragedies, particularly deception, seduction, and adultery with their consequences. In that case, *Anna Karenina* by Leo Tolstoy, *Adolphe* by Benjamin Constant, and *Casanova in Bolzano*, also known as *The Lover of Bolzano* by Sándor Márai, are included.

Following this section, a chapter discusses the

role of the "innocent" or "naive" in the novels, since seduced individuals, regardless of gender, are often portrayed as naive. Innocence implies a lack of worldly experience, openness, and purity, while naivety suggests unawareness or gullibility about relationship complexities and potential dangers. Voltaire's *Candide*, whose name embodies purity and honesty, embarks on a journey that both loses and warns against blindly accepting beliefs.

A section is included to discuss the culture of the walker or walks, mentioning Thomas Hardy's novels and the splendorous landscapes that his characters experience traveling through the English countryside and travel books.

In the chapter of *Death and Those Who Face It*, we use Seneca, *Letters on Ethics*, Montaigne's *Essays*. Also works of Spinoza, Schopenhauer, Tolstoy, Thomas Mann, and Irvin Yalom who's ideas included those that deal with a relevant theme for understanding human nature.

In the section "*The Terrorist,*" two masterpieces by Joseph Conrad are reviewed: "*Under Western Eyes*" and "*The Secret Agent,*" both written more than a hundred years ago, and whose fanatic characters use terror to promote their interests or those of the groups and governments that manipulate them. This section references the complex and controversial novel "*The Demons,*" also translated as "*The Possessed*" by Fyodor Dostoyevsky, in which the main character, an anarchist, and the group of nihilists that surround him, who come from the most diverse social classes in 19th-century Russia, are vividly represented with their great rawness.

There is a section looking at the diplomatic character, which does not apply exclusively to people who are formally appointed as a representative in a particular country or in an international organization. Diplomatic people are polite and avoid conflicts. They are attentive to others. In that section, we look for historical figures who laid the groundwork for diplomacy before it was formally recognized as an official title or profession in 1835 by the French Academy. Niccolò Machiavelli's seminal work, "*The Prince,*" is a notable example of a work that directly links to diplomacy, beyond mere power considerations.

Wealth, influence, and fame, archetypes in numerous famous novels, serve important narrative functions, representing themes of power, corruption, responsibility, and the human condition. They reflect society's complex relationship with wealth and influence, embodying aspirations for success and fears of power concentration. Among the many novels dealing with these themes, we selected Anthony Trollope's *The Way We Live Now*, a satirical critique of Victorian society's relentless pursuit of money, power, and social status. We also include in this section, *The Great Gatsby*, in which F. Scott Fitzgerald masterfully portrays money as a corrupting force, showing how it distorts the moral compass of individuals. The novel explores how both "old money" and "new money" contribute to moral decay, revealing the destructive nature of wealth. In another time and genre, William Shakespeare's *King Lear* presents another stark depiction of how wealth and power erode familial bonds and incite madness.

Under the heading *The Friends*, a set of books with selections of letters written by famous people are reviewed, such as those of Thomas Mann and Hermann Hesse, two great Nobel Prize winners in literature, the letters of the famous Russian author Lou-Andreas Salomé with the poet Rainer Maria Rilke, those exchanged by Vita Sackville-West and Virginia Woolf, and others.

Finally, a section on *Solitude* or *The Solitary* is included, highlighting *Crime and Punishment* by Fyodor Dostoyevsky, *The Notebooks of Malte Laurids Brigge*, Rilke's book/diary, *The Fall* by Albert Camus, and the controversial novel by Michel Houellebecq, *Submission*.

The archetype of the "guide" or "mentor" is easily recognizable in literature, particularly Virgil in Dante's *The Divine Comedy* exemplifies this role. As Dante's guide through Hell and Purgatory, Virgil leads him towards salvation. Among many other work included in this chapter Charles Dickens novels often included characters who serve as wise counselors, offering guidance, moral clarity, or practical advice to protagonists facing adversity.

Exile is often used in plots because it operates on multiple levels: geographical, social, psychological, and spiritual. This is especially evident in our hyper-connected social media landscape, where many individuals grapple with loneliness and alienation, even within their homes or countries.

To comprehend the essence of exile or the definition of an outsider, Odysseus emerges as a multifaceted character, embodying both the roles of exile and outsider throughout *The Odyssey* and its associated Greek myths. Albert Camus's *The Stranger* and James Joyce's *Exiles* are among other works we use since both clearly and figuratively represent this type of character.

Obsessive characters in literature illuminate the complexities of human nature. Driven by a singular pursuit, they often self-destruct, exploring the precarious balance between passion and obsession. Miguel de Cervantes' *Don Quixote* presents obsession in a unique perspective as is Captain Ahab from Herman Melville's *Moby Dick* who is consumed by an insatiable desire for revenge against the white whale.

Jealousy, envy, and hate are inherent human traits that have been explored in literature and philosophy. Spinoza's *Ethics* describes these emotions as a "vacillation" between love and hate for the same object, usually an individual. This arises when an individual imagines their beloved is united with another, leading to envy of the rival and animosity toward the beloved. Shakespeare's *Othello* stands as a quintessential exploration of this theme. Dostoevsky's *The Idiot* and Chekhov's *The Duel* masterfully portray envy as a festering undercurrent of intellectualism.

Finally we add the figure of the "solitary" which is a frequently used in novels and plays. Solitude is exemplified in Fyodor Dostoevsky's *Crime and Punishment,* where the protagonist's personality has been studied from a psychoanalytic perspective, particularly the origins of his early-life loneliness. Another example is Rilke's *The Notebooks of Malte Laurids Brigge,* a diary that reveals the narrator's loneliness as he observes people in Paris and on park benches, feeling disconnected from them. Albert Camus, one of the most influential French existentialist writers who has managed to apply literary talent to philosophy. In many of his works like *The Fall* and *The Stranger* it is possible to discover a nostalgic solitary.

I. Destructive Passions

Destructive relationships, in Freud's theory, occur when the death drive overrides the life instinct (Eros), causing individuals to repeat harmful patterns despite awareness of the damage—repetition compulsion. This self-destruction may manifest as aggression or sabotage in relationships and be worsened by unresolved unconscious conflicts.

Carl Jung explains destructive relationships through projection, the shadow, and individuation difficulties. When people enter relationships, they unconsciously project their denied qualities onto their partners, creating idealized or demonized dynamics fueled by unresolved personal conflicts.

Erich Fromm views destructiveness in relationships as influenced by both individual biology and social conditions. He identifies sadistic (domination, control, inflicting pain) and masochistic (submission, seeking control) tendencies as opposing forces in unhealthy relationships.

Irvin Yalom, an existential therapist, describes destructive relationships as "deficiency love," where one partner uses the other to fill their own sense of lack or isolation. Refusal to accept existential isolation leads to possessiveness or dependency, harming both partners.

The Obsessed [How singleminded pursuit destroys]

Obsessive characters in literature serve as a lens through which to examine the complexities of human nature. These individuals, driven by a singular pursuit—whether it be revenge, love, or ambition—often travel a path of self-destruction. Through these characters, literature explores the precarious equilibrium between passion and obsession, providing readers with a glimpse into the darker side of the human condition.

Miguel de Cervantes' *Don Quixote* presents obsession in a unique perspective—the fixation on an unattainable ideal. Don Quixote's obsession reading too many romance books with chivalric romances leads him to reject reality entirely. He becomes so engrossed in these narratives that "his humors became imbalanced, and he became convinced that all the books were accurate."

Don Quixote's obsession propels him to "reject the mundane everyday world he is familiar with" in favor of a fantastical realm where he can embody the role of a knight-errant. His single-minded pursuit of an unattainable ideal exemplifies how obsession can be both noble in its intentions and, regrettably, lead to tragic consequences in practice.

Sancho, Don Quixote's squire, too, harbors obsessive ambitions, fueled by his time alongside his presumptions knight. He dreams of governing his own "island," a fantasy ignited by his master's tales, and even envisions his daughter elevated to the title of duchess. Such aspirations seem unlikely to arise spontaneously in a simple man like Sancho; it is Don Quixote who has planted these grand desires within his impressionable mind. An obsessive mind can be contagious, spreading its intricate patterns and fixations to those nearby subtly altering perceptions and behaviors. What begins as mere curiosity can morph into an all-consuming quest, fueled by relentless focus and unwavering determination.

One of the most iconic examples of obsession in literature is Captain Ahab from Herman Melville's *Moby Dick*. Consumed by an insatiable desire for revenge against the white whale that took his leg, Ahab sacrifices his crew, his ship, and ultimately his own life in pursuit of his singular goal. His obsession blinds him to reason, transforming him into a tragic figure whose fixation leads to destruction. Ahab's relentless pursuit of Moby Dick serves as a cautionary tale about the dangers of unchecked obsession and the destructive power of revenge.

Another notable example is Edgar Allan Poe's novel "*The Tell-Tale Heart*," in which the protagonist is consumed by an irrational fear of an elderly man's eye. As the narrator descends into madness, he ultimately commits murder and succumbs to paranoia. The fixation on the eye serves as a metaphor for the protagonist's internal turmoil and guilt, underscoring how obsession can distort perception and lead to self-destructive behavior.

Emily Brontë's *Wuthering Heights* presents an intense portrayal of obsessive love through Heathcliff and Catherine Earnshaw. Their relationship demonstrates how obsession can span generations and destroy multiple lives. Heathcliff's "obsessive love for Catherine is the single principle of his being", a passion so overwhelming that it seems "insufficient and improper to call it love". Heathcliff's world shrinks, and Catherine becomes the sole object of his affection, leaving him incapable of caring for anyone else. This singular focus transforms him from a sympathetic figure into a brooding and destructive force.

Vladimir Nabokov's *Lolita* presents one of literature's most unsettling obsessions through Humbert Humbert's fixation on young girls, particularly Lolita Haze. Humbert's obsession transcends mere attraction; it becomes "physically and intellectually obsessive." He endeavors to "perpetually grasp the perilous enchantment of nymphets," illustrating how obsession can lead individuals to regard others as objects to be possessed rather than human beings.

The novel looks into themes of artistic and sexual obsession, implying that Humbert's perversity and his artistic abilities are intrinsically linked to an obsessive fixation on minutiae. His narration elucidates how obsession can distort perception and rationalize heinous actions, rendering him a fundamentally unreliable narrator whose "myopic self-deception and propensity for sympathy render numerous of his statements questionable."

Humbert, consumed by infatuation during his teenage years for the youthful Annabel Leigh, develops an enduring obsession. His yearning for women akin to Annabel results in unsuccessful marriages with mature women, as he attempts to suppress his desires, yet his obsession persists. This unfulfilled longing profoundly influences his tragic trajectory.

The Jealous, Envious and the Hater
[Scapegoating]

Spinoza, the renowned Dutch philosopher, in Part III of his seminal work *Ethics, On the Origin and Nature of the Affects*, presents a sweeping psychological theory. This theory categorizes forty-nine diverse human characters based on their unique interplay between emotions and reason. Spinoza doesn't offer rigid personality classifications; instead, he identifies core patterns of human existence stemming from emotional engagement and rational comprehension.

Regarding Jealousy, Spinoza thinks that it is a multifaceted emotion characterized by a "vacillation" or oscillation between love and hate directed toward the same object, typically an individual. This arises when an individual imagines that the object of their love is united with another by a stronger bond, resulting in both envy of the rival and animosity toward the beloved: "The hate of the loved object together with envy is jealousy, which is a vacillation, a combined love and hatred" (Ethics III, 35, Note). Jealousy thus combines the pain of envy (at the rival's good fortune) and the pain of hate (toward the beloved for perceived betrayal), resulting in emotional turmoil.

Spinoza defines envy as a specific form of hatred: it's "hatred that causes sadness at another's good fortune and joy at their evil." Hate, for Spinoza, is "pain with the idea of an external cause." When we perceive something as diminishing our power, we experience hate. Hate is linked to our desires and perceived threats to our well-being. Spinoza observes that hate intensifies with reciprocation, leading to cycles of hostility.

The progression from jealousy, desire, and envy to hatred and scapegoating is a damaging pattern in human behavior. Social comparison triggers feelings of inadequacy or resentment, leading to desire for others' possessions, status, or relationships. Envy intensifies these feelings, creating bitterness and resentment towards perceived advantages. As these emotions fester, they morph into hate, characterized by intense dislike and a desire to harm. Scapegoating displaces blame and responsibility, targeting individuals or groups for pent-up anger. This cycle perpetuates conflict, erodes social bonds, and inflicts lasting psychological wounds.

Scapegoating theory suggests that prejudiced individuals view themselves as victims and blame vulnerable groups. Hitler's actions exemplify this, leading to discriminatory laws and mass extermination. He exploited Jewish people as a scapegoat for Germany's social and economic problems in the 1930s. This pattern of envious admiration and resentment appears to have characterized his relationship with successful Jewish individuals and the Jewish community.

Analyzing these four interwoven themes—jealousy, envy, hatred, and scapegoating—has provided the foundation for compelling literature throughout history. These themes serve as potent driving forces, illuminating the most profound aspects of human nature while delving into intricate moral and societal dilemmas.

French philosopher and literary critic René Girard delves into the intricate relationship between jealousy, hate, and scapegoating in his profound analysis. His theory posits that mimetic desire serves as the underlying mechanism, providing a unique framework for comprehending the interwoven nature of these destructive character traits. Girard's insights, while echoed and critiqued by other scholars, illuminate the intricate emotional dynamics that underpin human rivalry and social conflict.

His mimetic theory shows how human desires are imitated from others, leading to rivalry, conflict, and, ultimately, the scapegoating of individuals or groups to restore social order. His theory has been widely applied to understanding the mechanisms behind violence, including the mass scapegoating seen in Nazi Germany.

Girard's theory of the scapegoat offers a crucial lens for examining the inner workings of Nazism. Societies grappling with internal strife often find relief by scapegoating individuals or groups, attributing societal problems to them, and expelling or eliminating them to restore order. Girard made reference to the Nazi regime's systematic persecution and extermination of Jewish people to explain this phenomenon. Facing widespread social and economic instability, the Nazis successfully mobilized the German populace by blaming Jews for Germany's misfortunes, leading to unimaginable acts of violence.

Girard's formative years were shaped by the Nazi occupation of France. He experienced firsthand the humiliation, fear, and social fragmentation that occupation brought, witnessing how suspicion and accusation divided communities. These experiences deeply influenced his later work on mobs, hate, violence, rivalry, and scapegoating.

Regarding fiction, Shakespeare's *Othello* stands as a quintessential exploration of this theme, wherein Iago's professional jealousy, stemming from being overlooked for promotion, metamorphoses into a malevolent plot to destroy Othello through fabricated suspicions of infidelity. This initial spark of envy ignites a pervasive web of deceit, exploiting Othello's vulnerabilities and ultimately resulting in the downfall of both Othello and Desdemona. Iago masterfully exploits Othello's trusting nature, weaving a web of circumstantial evidence and carefully planted suggestions that prey on Othello's deepest fears. The green-eyed monster, as Iago calls it, consumes Othello, blinding him to reason and driving him to commit an act of irreversible violence. The tragedy of Othello serves as a stark warning about the destructive power of unchecked jealousy and its capacity to corrupt even the noblest of souls.

Russian literature has been particularly masterful at exploring envy's psychological depths. In Dostoevsky's *The Idiot*, the character Rogozhin is described as "jealousy personified," displaying "so many shades of jealousy and pain." The novel demonstrates how envy can take over, shaping a person's whole being. Envy manifests not just as a fleeting emotion but as a persistent state of mind, influencing actions, relationships, and overall perception of the world.

In Chekhov's *The Duel*, Ivan Laevsky embodies

a subtle yet destructive form of envy, targeting those he perceives as more successful or content, leading to profound inadequacy and self-loathing. Chekhov masterfully portrays this envy as festering beneath intellectualism, poisoning Laevsky's relationships and hindering his growth. Laevsky's antagonism with Von Koren highlights an ideological clash. Laevsky, the "superfluous man" intellectual, blames external circumstances for his failures, attributing them to literary influences like Onegin, Pechorin, and Bazarov rather than taking responsibility. Von Koren, representing Social Darwinism and scientific rationalism, views Laevsky as "absolutely pernicious" and believes eliminating him would be a service. Von Koren's harsh judgment stems from his belief in natural selection and his conviction that weak individuals like Laevsky should be eliminated for society's benefit.

Seeking a nuanced perspective on blame and animosity, Nathaniel Hawthorne's seminal novel, *The Scarlet Letter*, employs the character of Hester Prynne as both a literal and metaphorical scapegoat. Hester Prynne, a literary icon, stands as a scapegoat for adultery, though her partner remains unpunished. Hester becomes the sole moral judge in her Puritan community, critiquing the harshness of society and the unfair blame women faced for men's sins. Despite pressure and rejection, Hester transcends her role as a scapegoat, becoming a symbol of strength, independence, and redemption.

Hawthorne's narrative highlights the human tendency to find a single target for widespread problems, suggesting that blaming an individual is easier than confronting deeper societal issues. The author's character embodies the idea that scapegoats are frequently drawn from groups that are already vulnerable due to their gender, economic standing, or place in society.

These themes also resonate in contemporary science fiction literature and gaming. J. R. R. Tolkien's works, particularly *The Hobbit* and *The Lord of the Rings*, are renowned for their exploration of issues such as envy, hatred, and scapegoating. In Tolkien's world, objects like the Arkenstone and the One Ring become focal points of mimetic desire using the René Girard ideas. For instance, Thorin's desire for the "Arkenstone," a legendary precious gemstone, extends beyond its monetary value. It embodies the symbolism of kingship and power, and he perceives others, such as Smaug and Bilbo, also seeking it, which engenders rivalry and envy among those who covet it. The Ring itself is a powerful object of desire. It corrupts by amplifying the bearer's desire for power, making others want to possess it, mirroring the desires of those around them.

Tolkien uses scapegoating to bring rival groups together. The Dwarves, Elves, and Men forget their quarrels and unite against the Goblins, who become the common enemy and scapegoat for all their anger and conflict. This aligns with Girard's concept that a crisis of rivalry is resolved by directing collective anger toward an innocent third party, as a scapegoat who serves as a unifying force, enabling otherwise divided groups to transcend their internal conflicts and concentrate on a shared adversary.

Seducer/Seduced

The character of the seducer is generally instinctively associated with Don Juan and Casanova and, in many cases, with the generic Playboy. Among the multiple authors who use the figure of Don Juan, Mozart's opera of the same name stands out, the poems of Lord Byron and Guillaume Baudelaire, the plays of Molière, Juan Zorrilla, Miguel de Unamuno, Jacinto Benavente, and Ingmar Bergman, the novels of Azorín, Peter Handke, Apollinaire, Luis Spota, and José Saramago, as well as the films of Salvador Toscano and Roger Badin. This list is arbitrary and certainly lacks dozens of works that, without using Don Juan in their title, are interpretations of the famous seducer.

Besides *Don Juan,* there are numerous books, novels, texts, and manuals that deal with the conduct or phenomenon of the seducer from different angles. This qualifier or conduct generally refers to men, despite the fact that there have been and are famous seductresses. Cleopatra stands out, who, with her beauty, enchanted Caesar and later Mark Antony. Cleopatra has been represented by prestigious artists in paintings, sculptures, plays, novels, and films. The famous tragedy *Antony and Cleopatra* by William Shakespeare, George Frideric Handel's opera *Julius Caesar in Egypt,* and in cinema *Cleopatra* starring Elizabeth Taylor in 1963 stand out. Another famous and recognized seductress is Margaretha Geertruida MacLeod, better known as Mata Hari, whose eventful life as a spy during World War I inspired several films, including one starring Greta Garbo in 1932.

One of the most recognized books on the subject is *Diary of a Seducer* by the famous 19th-century Danish philosopher and theologian Søren Kierkegaard. The work describes the desire of the narrator, called Juan, like the famous prototype of the seducer Don Juan, who designs a strategy to make Cordelia, the female character, fall in love and finally obtain her favors.

Kierkegaard's book describes the main character's reflections on the art of seduction and transcribes diary entries and letters that Juan writes to the target of his conquest, in which he tests his methods and theories. In the letters, Kierkegaard shows the steps Juan follows to manipulate Cordelia and finally conquer her and thus achieve his goal of possessing her. In these letters it is possible to distinguish machination, persuasion, and finally fabrication. Cordelia's responses, on the other hand, project resentment for being seduced and subsequently abandoned, but at the same time reveal the hope of recovering lost love.

Among the dozens of books on seduction, *The Art of Seduction* by Robert Greene stands out, which without being a manual explores the concept using historical figures like Cleopatra and Casanova. *The Art of Seduction* follows the successful work by the same author, *The 48 Laws of Power*, since Greene considers seduction as another manifestation of power. The book is divided by categories or types of seducers including an "anti-seducer" and different types of victims, supported by concrete examples of historical figures. Additionally, Greene describes what he calls seduction techniques to make someone fall under the spell.

Among the classic novels that show the prototype of the seducer, *Adolphe* by 19th-century writer Benjamin Constant stands out. First published in London and Paris in 1816, the book captivated numerous academics and romantic readers in different languages. For example, in 2002, French director Benoît Jacquot adapted *Adolphe* into a film starring the famous actress Isabelle Adjani.

Benjamin Constant was born in Lausanne, Switzerland, and is better known for his books on politics. He was an active liberal political figure at the end of the French Revolution, as a member of the Directory in 1799 and later of the "Tribunal," but was forced to resign by Napoleon Bonaparte for his radical ideas about democratic rules, as well as the usurpation of power, concepts that form the core of his writings.

Some believe that *Adolphe* is an autobiographical novel, since Constant was also a seducer in real life. Like Adolphe, he also pursued women older than him, particularly married women neglected by their husbands, who tend to be vulnerable from an emotional point of view, making them easy prey for skilled lovers.

Constant had a 15-year romantic relationship with Germaine de Staël, with whom in addition to the emotional bond he also had great affinity in political matters. Constant was forced into exile and to leave Napoleon's Paris to settle at Château de Coppet, property of the Staël family, located near Geneva, where she organized famous salon-style gatherings, attended by refugees and political thinkers to discuss international events. Before Adolphe was published,

Mme. de Staël had written two novels that can be seen as an "inverse mirror" of Constant's novel, since the victim is not a tormented married woman who falls madly in love with a younger and more selfish lover as in *Adolphe*, but rather a married man who falls in love with a woman who makes him suffer as seducers do. Like Constant, Mme. de Staël also used the proper names of the main characters as titles of the novels: *Corinne* (1802) and *Delphine* (1807).

Adolphe is written in the form of a young man's diary, whose text is sent in a wooden box by an innkeeper to an editor who was stranded at his inn by a snowstorm. The contents of the mysterious box are described by the editor as "a quantity of very old letters, either without address or in which the addresses and signatures were illegible, the portrait of a woman and a notebook containing the story."

Adolphe, the novel's narrator, recalls his father's decision to send him on a tour of Europe at twenty-two. He fell in love with Ellénore, a married woman ten years his senior.

Adolphe enjoyed his adventure of seduction, describing his friends' delight in his conquest of Ellénore's husband and their imitation of him.

Ellénore feels the opposite upon realizing that "opinion was turning against her." Female friends, "break the connection with the greatest possible ostentation." Men, on the other hand, "came . . . because she was still attractive and her recent fragility had given them aspirations that they made no effort to disguise."

Adolphe's happy adventure soon turns to misfortune and social isolation. His father, concerned about his son's future, breaks their relationship. Bored, Adolphe seeks to end the emotional and social burden of the adventure. The book focuses on Ellénore's desperate feelings as she watches her beloved distance himself, almost cruelly. Adolphe realizes Ellénore has sacrificed everything for him, now socially isolated and deeply in love. He understands that a separation would cause her pain and lead to his lover's suicide.

Benjamin Constant in this brief novel explores with considerable knowledge the social context in post-French Revolution Europe and shows a deep understanding of individual feelings and the psychological mental state of those who confuse love with infatuation. His novel deals with unhealthy relationships pursued by immature egocentric seducers who target fragile people, who always suffer tragic endings, since most of the time, seducers, once they achieve their conquests, cease to be the solicitous lover.

There are many novels that follow the same pattern, such as *Senso*, written by Camillo Boito and adapted for cinema by Luchino Visconti in 1954.

Likewise, *The Ballad of the Sad Café* by Carson McCullers brilliantly portrays this type of relationship but in reverse, when it describes a love relationship that distinguishes the "lover" and the "beloved." Clearly, "the beloved is only a stimulus for all the stored love that has remained silent within the lover for a long time," which does not happen with the seducer, who is selfish and finally accumulates relationships that generally end in tragedy. The beloved, according to McCullers' novel, can be treacherous, deceitful and given to bad habits, and the lover can see this clearly but that does not affect the relationship or the love they feel for the beloved.

Anna Karenina shows us Tolstoy's obsessive eye on love, jealousy, adultery, and the decline of the Russian aristocracy. The novel possibly presents one of the clearest examples of the damage that an arrogant and selfish seducer can inflict on his lover or lovers. *War and Peace* and *Anna Karenina* are the most famous works of the famous Russian writer, the first published in 1869, the second published in installments from 1873 to 1877. They are regularly compared in terms of stylistic differences. For some scholars, the inclusion of essays in a narrative that tends to be fictional makes it difficult to categorize War and Peace as a novel. Tolstoy wrote an interpretive note titled "A Few Words about War and Peace" in which he explicitly confirmed that this work "is not a novel, much less a poem, and much less a historical chronicle." This explanation by the author makes *Anna Karenina* his first novel. Another important difference is the time when the two works take place. The events contained in *War and Peace* occur during the French invasion of Russia in 1812, while those presented in *Anna Karenina* correspond to the years in which it was written. As it is a series that was completed over several years, this allowed Tolstoy to witness and describe, through his characters, how Russian society was changing, including its ideas about its country and its own class.

Considered one of Tolstoy's masterpieces, *Anna Karenina* is recognized for its convincing character portraits and the extraordinary situations in the story. It has the characteristic style of the famous novelist, which allows readers to explore the complex personalities of the characters, and also analyze their desires, ideas, tastes, and most intimate emotions.

The novel is full of interesting dialogues and conversations on various topics, ranging from the most frivolous gossip to sophisticated themes such as education, religion, morality, politics, etc.

One of the characteristics of Tolstoy's novels is creating believable characters with whom readers quickly identify, describing their actions in detail. His way of writing is an invitation for readers to witness and be able to share the atmosphere of different situations, such as attending events, a ball, a concert, a dinner, a hunt or a horse race. His rich language helps us discover where his ideological affinities and antipathies respectively lie. Many times his characters pose as part of himself, or are inspired by close friends or family members, making his novels to some extent autobiographical, especially when he makes the character and ideas of Konstantin Levin, one of the main characters in the story, a kindred soul to the author.

The novel also highlights the situations of the arrogant aristocracy in decline, challenged by only a minority of progressive reformers, as well as the growing "nouveau riche" who embrace luxuries and a colorful lifestyle. Some members of the old world aristocracy are struggling to maintain their expensive standard of living by increasing their debts and rapidly diminishing inheritances or income from land.

There is also another type of aristocrat who can be content with a simple life. They are genuinely concerned with the problems faced by peasants and think that land is a relatively important issue in Russia compared to the rest of Europe.

Tolstoy also shows the double morality of the high society of Moscow and Petersburg, which ostracizes the heroine Anna, who chooses to sacrifice her honor and her family for love.

After finishing the last chapters of *Anna Karenina*, Tolstoy renounced his aristocratic background and focused on "morally uplifting tales." He published dozens of pamphlets and essays promoting Christian values in an attempt to encourage social change. Two years after *Anna Karenina* was published in 1889, Tolstoy finished *The Kreutzer Sonata*, initially banned, a novel that was considered one of the best books about jealousy and sexual obsession. Many critics think it matches *Othello* by William Shakespeare, *The Eternal Husband* by Fyodor Dostoyevsky, *Tess of the d'Urbervilles* by Thomas Hardy, and many other great novels or plays that deal with these complex, dark emotional attributes of destructive human relationships.

In *Anna Karenina*, infidelity or adultery is one of the central themes, entangled with jealousy. It is possible to find some similarities between *Anna Karenina* and other 19th-century romantic novels in which certain heroines are married to an older man with high positions in society and break their marriages by fatally falling in love with young officers. As an avid reader of French literature and politics, Tolstoy was familiar with and probably read *Adolphe*, Benjamin Constant's classic novel previously reviewed. In both stories, the heroine falls in love with a young, handsome, and vain officer—Anna with Vronsky and Ellénor with Adolphe. Both renounce their stable and privileged status and abandon their husbands. They lose a comfortable life and are rejected by society. However, the similarities end there, as the stories develop in a different way.

Anna is not abandoned by her suitor, while Ellénore is. Although proud of his conquest, Vronsky is captivated by Anna's beauty and personality, so he pursues her ardently, regardless of the consequences of getting involved with a married woman. He makes no excuses and wants to live with Anna and even proposes marriage to her. Adolphe, on the other hand, boasts of his conquest and enjoys the fame acquired for his skill in having supplanted Ellénore's husband.

However, for Anna, the consequences are enormous, over the sacrifice of leaving her beloved son and her comfortable social position. Unlike the admiration that the seducer Vronsky awakens, Anna is marginalized by society and most of her "friends," who turn their backs on her and criticize her harshly. Tolstoy's description of the harsh responses to Anna's conduct shows one of the darkest sides of the Russian aristocracy.

Many critical characters are not included in this review, as in the case of Anna's husband, whose anger and dilemmas face the sentimental adventure of his loyal wife seduced by a young cadet, since the idea is to point out the character of the seducer and the tragic outcomes that pursue their victims like Anna Karenina. Despite the fact that these classic novels take place in distant and far-off cultures and times, they contain aspects of universal character and therefore are reproduced with different nuances, but the characters and situations remain the same.

Casanova is another name associated with the seducer, whose characteristics are defined at the beginning of this category of human behavior. Unlike Don Juan, who is a generic name used as a stereotype of a shameless seducer, Giacomo Casanova was a real-life character born in Venice in 1725. At that time Venice was famous for being a libertine city whose famous Carnival attracted tourists from the most diverse countries. His mother was a famous actress and his father a dancer and also an actor. The family context and the atmosphere of a disordered Venice with visitors of the most diverse origin possibly explain his libertine character as well as the frugal relationships with women described in his famous autobiography, *Histoire de ma vie* (*History of My Life*), which is considered one of the most authoritative sources on the customs and norms of European social life during the 18th century.

Casanova's name has become so famous for his often complicated and elaborate affairs with women that his name is now synonymous with "libertine." He spent the last years of his life at Dux Chateau (Bohemia) as a librarian in the house of Count Waldstein, where he also wrote his autobiography.

Hungarian novelist Sándor Marai published in 1940 the novel *Vendégjáték Bolzanóban* (*Guest Game in Bolzano*), translated into English as *Casanova in Bolzano* in 2001. The book is written in a style that allows recognition from the first pages of the character of the famous Italian seducer, particularly the charisma he exploits to extract all kinds of benefits, including money, favors from women and particularly fame that represents the key that opens all kinds of doors for him.

Casanova escapes from a Venice prison and arrives in Bolzano, where he stays at a boarding house. Despite his rags, they give him the most expensive room, openly acknowledging his poverty and only possession: a Venetian dagger. Marai describes the town's women's reactions, comparing him to other men and saying: "There are cunning, vociferous, gallant men who exaggerate their feelings, indifferent, timid, and boring ones . . . None are real men." Upon seeing him, they understood his fame and the unrest in the city, reacting with blinking, sighing, panting, and chest pressing.

Like the real Casanova, Marai's character is a poet and writer who considers writing the most powerful force, surpassing even the pope, king, and dux. Marai dedicates a chapter to celebrating the power of writing and the privilege of the writer, echoing the novelist's sentiments.

Clearly, being a writer is not an attribute of the conventional seducer, although poets, musicians, novelists, and artists in general have a reputation for having a special élan or attractiveness that in many cases is used to obtain favors in the sentimental field.

Marai's novel portrays Casanova as a sophisticated seducer, not only for his literary prowess, as the author of the famous *"Memoirs of Casanova,"* but also for his mentor, a Venetian senator who finances his excesses and pays his gambling debts unconditionally. Upon arriving in Bolzano, Casanova receives a large sum of money to pay for his boarding house and buy an expensive trousseau, improving his image and enhancing his seduction skills.

The central element in the novel is a supposed relationship with Francesca, the wife of an old Count of Parma, relative of the King of France who in the past wounded him to death in a duel, but for some unknown reason, the Count saves his life.

After several years, the three meet in the same city. The Count, who was aware of Casanova's arrival in Bolzano (despite having promised that he would kill him if he saw the countess again), makes a surprising visit to the inn where the seducer is staying. He wants to save his wife from disappointment and suffering since he is convinced that like any seduction the adventure is temporary, would last only a few days and nights "in which she would be yours; you would only give her an indifferent tenderness, a fire that burns but does not warm."

The novel is essentially a duel in which the Count of Parma, with the weapons of a loving husband, tests the seducer by challenging him to reveal himself and prove whether his wife is loyal to him or not. It is a triangle that is resolved by testing the seducer's tricks and wiles.

To move to another time and Latinoamérica fiction, *Casi el paraíso* by Luis Spota stands out among Mexican novels with characters inspired by Casanova. The central character, Ugo Conti, shares similarities with Casanova, including being Italian. Ugo Conti, the bastard son of an Italian prostitute, becomes a refined seducer of mature and rich women using a false noble title. An Austrian or German countess who knows his past gives him the script to act and behave like a "prince" and baptizes him Prince Hugo Conti, whom she considers "The most beautiful man and like Casanova the most perverse."

Spota's novel recounts his exploits, taking him to exclusive places and luxurious yachts to Acapulco and later to Mexico City among the wealthy. He exploits them sexually and economically, receiving millionaire loans to recover his lost invented fortune during the war and awaiting a lawsuit.

There is no doubt that it is difficult to present a single prototype of the seducer. The one represented by the aforementioned *Adolphe* by Benjamin Constant is different from Vronsky, *Anna Karenina*'s lover, and from Hugo Conti by Mexican writer Luis Spota, who is more interested in money and fame than in conquering women. Finally, Marai presents us with a duel between the Duke of Alba, Francesca's husband, who apparently tests Casanova's powers of seduction.

In our time, while it is true that the pathetic conduct of seduction and deception to obtain favors from the unwary has not disappeared, fortunately it has become evident that, in addition to the seducer's persuasive power—exercising abuse from a hierarchical position of power in an institution, there are people who use this conduct to force their victims to comply with their whims against their will. There are dozens of examples that have been made public of this horrifying abuse among those who fortunately have received deserved punishment and tarnished their careers. The cases of Harvey Weinstein, the famous film producer, Plácido Domingo in music, and recently Luis Rubiales in Spanish football stand out. These examples are of famous public figures who were denounced and represent a very low percentage of this type of abuse that, in addition to being a crime, in most cases goes unpunished.

Impossible not to include in this section is Stendhal's *The Red and the Black,* a classic novel, dealing with the complex mix of seduction, ambition, and desire for social advancement within the rigid societal structure of post-Napoleonic France. Julian Sorel, the main protagonist, is a young man of humble origins who aspires to social advancement. In pursuit of this goal, he enters the intricate and competitive realm of love and power. Julian employs his intelligence, charm, and cunning as tools to secure employment as a mentor to the children of prominent members of the society of a small town. In this capacity, as a means of asserting his ascendancy, he seduces Mme de Rênal, the wife of his initial employer.

Subsequently, he moves to Paris as the private secretary of the Marquis de la Mole, a significant advancement in the capital's aristocratic world. Living in the same premises gives him the chance to pursue Mathilde, the Marquis's daughter. After initially succumbing to Julien, who is left despondent and unsure how to win her back, Julien seeks the advice of Prince Korasoff, a Russian nobleman. Korasoff becomes his confidant and offers Julien a strategic piece of seduction advice: "feign interest in another woman within Mathilde's social circle to provoke her jealousy and reignite her passion. As an expert seducer, akin to Søren Kierkegaard, Casanova, and other authors previously mentioned, Korasoff's counsel to Julien revolves around manipulating Mathilde's emotional state by instilling uncertainty regarding Julien's genuine feelings for her.

The Innocent/Naif

As in the novels quoted before, in cultural stereotypes and psychological analyses, seduced individuals, regardless of gender, are often portrayed as naive or innocent. Innocence suggests a lack of worldly experience, openness, and purity, while naivety implies unawareness or gullibility concerning the complexities and potential dangers in relationships and intentions.

The perfect example of this type of character is Voltaire's *Candide*, whose name itself implies purity and honesty, embarking on a journey that serves as both a loss of innocence and a warning against blindly accepting beliefs without question. These experiences challenge the protagonist's naivety, forcing him to confront the harsh realities of the world and question the optimistic philosophies he once embraced.

Candide's naivety in life shapes his interactions and decisions with a boyish trust that makes him vulnerable to the harsh reality of human selfishness.

He accepts the goodwill of others, a trait that leads him into the hands of exploiters and deceivers time and again. Even amidst a torrent of misfortunes Candide clings to Pangloss's optimistic teachings. This unwavering faith often blinds him to the lessons of experience, preventing him from forming his own independent judgments and perpetuating a cycle of naive missteps.

Over the novel, Candide's innocence is gradually eroded by the world's brutality and absurdity. Voltaire uses his journey as a metaphor for the loss of innocence from experience and exposure to real-world suffering. Initially naive and sheltered in Baron Thunder-ten-tronckh's castle, Candide witnesses horrific events like war, natural disasters, betrayal, personal loss, and human cruelty.

Dostoevsky's *The Idiot* stands as another significant classic novel, featuring a character named Prince Myshkin, who embodies innocence more profoundly than naivety. He is a figure of significant moral innocence, embodying goodness, compassion, and a selfless nature. This contrasts sharply with the corrupt and cynical society that surrounds him. His innocence isn't due to a lack of intelligence or awareness. Instead, it is a deep purity, as he refuses to participate in the manipulations and self-serving behaviors of those around him.

II. Travelers and Walkers

The conduct of a traveler involves respectful, safe, and lawful behavior in all destinations, showing regard for the people, cultures, and environments encountered along the journey. A traveler is expected to comply not only with local laws but also with standards aimed at ensuring mutual respect and positive experiences for everyone involved.

A walker—often synonymous with a pedestrian—is a person who moves on foot, whether for commuting, recreation, or exploration. The conduct of a walker similarly entails behaving with awareness for surroundings, observing local customs such as appropriate use of sidewalks or footpaths, and maintaining safety and courtesy toward others sharing the same spaces.

Before horses or other draft animals were used to transport human beings, walking was a necessity and the only option for moving from one place to another. Pilgrimages to holy places or to participate in religious festivals continue to be another manifestation of the act of walking. In our times, walking is an exercise or pastime that takes different forms such as relaxed strolls for contemplating places of natural interest or for exploring streets, monuments, or historical spaces in cities.

Likewise, walking can take the character of casual walks for purposes of individual or collective reflection or have a romantic purpose. There have also been important walks of a political character between heads of state, particularly the famous so-called "walk in the woods" in 1982, when the distinguished American diplomat Paul Nitze undertook with the Soviet ambassador, Yuliy Kvitinsky, a walk that created the expectation of a thaw in the Cold War and which years later served as the basis for producing real progress in the disarmament process between the two main nuclear powers during the Reykjavik Summit of 1986.

Descriptions of famous walks taken by music composers like Gustav Mahler, who in the Austrian Alps took long walks in search of musical inspiration. Among the famous writers remembered as walkers, Johann Wolfgang Goethe stands out, which has given rise to numerous paths for walking enthusiasts bearing his name, such as the well-known "Thuringian Goethe" route that begins in the center of Weimar, where the famous writer established his residence, and ends at Belvedere Castle, which is the entry point for other multiple Goethe walks.

Perhaps one of the most popular tourist walks is that of the famous "Camino de Santiago," which was established after the discovery of the relics of Santiago the Great in the early 9th century. A few years later, it became an important pilgrimage route of Christianity. In our days, each year, nearly half a million pilgrims, Christians and laypeople of the most diverse nationalities, take walks along various routes that end at the Cathedral of Santiago de Compostela, where masses are celebrated daily.

It would be impossible to name all the writers

who describe paths and landscapes that characters traverse for different reasons in their novels. The famous Victorian novelist and poet Thomas Hardy stands out, who with great detail situates the paths traveled by the characters in his novels in an imaginary district in southeast England that he calls Wessex, inspired by the counties of Dorset, Wiltshire, Somerset, Devon, Hampshire, and Berkshire, in southwest and south-central England. In his most famous novels: *Tess of the d'Urbervilles, Far from the Madding Crowd,* and *Jude the Obscure,* the characters walk for entire days along beautifully described and detailed places in different seasons of the year, and the rich description he makes of the landscapes in the walks and the multiple strolls taken by the characters in his novels, including the rich details of their gardens, farms, and nature in general, allows the reader to be another walker and enjoy the landscape.

To give an idea of Hardy's descriptions, here is a passage chosen arbitrarily from the novel *Tess of the d'Urbervilles.* Hardy wrote: ". . . During this October month of marvelous afternoons, they wandered along the grassy plains, by creeping paths that followed the edge of streams, jumping across small wooden bridges to the other side, and back." The walks in his novels are so attractive that "The Thomas Hardy Society" offers to "explore the beautiful heart of Hardy country with a guided walk through Dorset" (https://www.hardysociety.org/resources/walks/).

There is also a long tradition of travel books and novels that the prestigious literary magazine

London Books Review publishes in a series of articles with reviews of books by authors who have written about the experience of walking, exploring, describing, or simply conversing while enjoying the landscape. In particular, the English writer Robert Macfarlane is a writer dedicated to writing about nature, the most diverse landscapes in places of particular beauty through which he has traveled. Nominated to receive the Nobel Prize in literature, his books have been widely recognized and received numerous awards. In addition to having walked in his country, England and Scotland, he describes his experiences in Spain, Palestine, and Tibet. His objective here is to describe some of his most memorable explorations through "pilgrim paths, green paths, guided paths, risky paths, etc."

There is a long tradition, and he mentions that walkers can be travelers for whom traveling is work (travelers, messengers, shepherds), or those with the taste or honor of reaching a goal (pilgrims, crusaders), or those who walk for the experience. Wordsworth and Coleridge did this, as did George Borrow, who captivated Victorian readers with his tales of Spain and Wales. In our time, Macfarlane notes, Patrick Leigh Fermor walked from Holland to the Balkans in the 1930s, and Rory Stewart (and his dog) walked through Afghanistan immediately after September 11th.

Leopold Bloom, the protagonist of James Joyce's novel *Ulysses*, embarks on a daily odyssey walking through the streets of Dublin on June 16, 1904, which serves as the narrative's central focus. His journey through the city mirrors Odysseus's epic wanderings but on a mundane, intimate scale. Joyce uses Bloom to explore themes of identity, alienation, and the search for meaning in everyday life. Bloom's walks are meticulously detailed, mirroring both the city's geography and the intricacy of his inner life. Although Bloom's errands—purchasing a kidney, attending a funeral, visiting the post office—appear ordinary, his path is frequently circuitous, reflecting both practical motives (such as avoiding acquaintances) and a deeper sense of disorientation or searching.

III. The Diplomats

The diplomatic character does not apply exclusively to people who are formally appointed by their government as a representative in a particular country or in an international organization. Those people whose conduct is conciliatory or polite are said to be diplomatic since they aim to avoid conflicts; their behavior is polite and attentive to others. These are some examples of stereotypical behaviors.

The word "diplomatic," to designate an official title or a profession, was not inscribed as such until 1835 in the sixth edition of the Dictionary of the French Academy. In 1798, the fifth edition presented the word "diplomacy" as a science—that is, knowledge or know-how—of relations and interests from power to power. The men who are present in negotiations or in defense of the interests of their states in congresses, summits, or conflicts are, therefore, men who are supposed to have the science or at least the practice.

Long before diplomacy was formally recognized as a distinct profession, several historical figures laid the groundwork for its practice and theory. Among the authors whose work is directly linked to the art of diplomacy, beyond the obvious considerations of power, stands Niccolò Machiavelli. In his seminal work, *The Prince, it* is easy to find early conceptions of the diplomat's role, particularly the need to have strategic thinking and negotiation skills, even if the approach can be viewed as ruthless or pragmatic.

Machiavelli has firsthand experience in the trade as a representative himself, serving as a key diplomat for the Republic from 1498 to 1512. He was responsible for the city-state's foreign affairs, which implied he was frequently sent on diplomatic missions throughout Italy and to major European powers, including France and the Holy Roman Empire.

In his writings, the Florentine emphasized the diplomat's primary function is to advocate for the interests of his own prince or state. Employing a parable, he emphasize the necessity of the diplomat to adapt to various circumstances. He mentions a "fox," characterized by cunning and the ability to discern traps, and a "lion," renowned for its strength and capacity to intimidate adversaries.

Machiavelli's writings emphasize the significance of comprehending the motivations and intentions of foreign rulers, a crucial skill. One of Machiavelli's primary objectives, which remains relevant to ambassadors and diplomats, is to establish connections at the highest levels of their host country. This involves not only engaging with government officials but also navigating private and cultural circles. Machiavelli's approach involves gathering information, making informed judgments, and effectively reporting to the home government.

Henry Kissinger, a diplomat himself as former U.S. National Security Advisor and Secretary of State wrote an important book titled *Diplomacy* in 1994. This comprehensive history of international relations, spanning from the 17th century in Europe through the World Wars and the Cold War, offers a detailed account of pivotal diplomatic

events. Notably, Henry Kissinger's personal negotiations with world leaders, such as the opening
relations with China and the conclusion of the war
in Vietnam, are provided in meticulous detail.

Another model that serves to understand the
role of a diplomat is provided by Isaiah Berlin,
the renowned British philosopher and historian of
ideas, who held the position of First Secretary of
the British Embassy in Washington from 1942 to
1945. In his book *Washington Dispatches, 1941–1945*
published by the University of Chicago, is a contemporary example of diplomatic conduct during
wartime since compiles Berlin's weekly political reports sent from the British Embassy in Washington,
DC, during World War. These dispatches provide
detailed analysis and commentary on American
politics, public opinion, and the evolving U.S.-
British relationship during a critical period, offering
a unique insights into wartime diplomacy.

There is the notion from Machiavelli that diplomacy includes formal or informal actions that could
fit the profile of spying. Many embassies employ
staff specifically dedicated to gathering information through various means, which can include
both overt and covert channels. These individuals
are tasked with staying informed about political,
economic, and social developments within the host
country, providing valuable insights to their home
government.

In the majority of John le Carré novels, characters
who assume dual roles profoundly intertwine with
the realm of diplomacy, serving both as a backdrop
and a thematic element. His stories often explore

the blurred boundaries between official diplomacy and covert intelligence work. John le Carré's first-hand experience as an intelligence officer for both MI5 and MI6 granted him an exclusive perspective on the intricate interplay between diplomacy and espionage.

Among Le Carré many spy novels, only a few present protagonists who explicitly assume dual roles as diplomats and spies. In *A Perfect Spy,* the protagonist, Magnus Pym, is a British intelligence officer who operates under diplomatic guise. While officially serving as a diplomat in Vienna, his role serves as a subterfuge for his espionage endeavors. The novel follows his double life as both a diplomat and a spy, ultimately revealing his work as a double agent for the Czechoslovak secret service.

In *The Russia House,* the protagonist Barley Blair, a book publisher, becomes entangled in British and American intelligence operations that use diplomatic channels and cover to facilitate espionage. Diplomats play crucial roles in running agents and managing intelligence, though Blair himself is drawn into the world of espionage. Like many of John le Carré's novels, the author conducted research trips to the depicted locations and established direct contacts with experts and individuals who inspired the characters. In the Introduction, Le Carré lists those who helped him in his research, including Strobe Talbott, a Sovietologist who became Deputy Secretary of State after the book's publication.

IV. Those Who Face Death

Facing death is a central theme for Albert Camus, Gustave Husserl, and Jacques Derrida, but each approaches it from a distinct philosophical perspective rooted in their core concepts and existential concerns.

Camus: Absurdity and Revolt. For Camus, death is the ultimate expression of life's absurdity—the abrupt end that contradicts the search for transcendent meaning or ultimate resolution. He argues that since there's nothing beyond this life and no hope of immortality, true wisdom lies in facing death lucidly, refusing resignation and religious consolation. Instead, his philosophy calls for revolt—a persistent, creative defiance that renders life valuable in the face of its absurdity. Death, for Camus, is to be held in conscious view: not denied or covered by hope, but confronted as the inescapable cessation of experience.

Husserl: Phenomenology, Interruption, and Threat. Edmund Husserl analyzes death phenomenologically, examining its disruption of life, projects, and meaning. He distinguishes several senses of death: natural end, historical event, interruption, and constant threat. From the living subject's perspective, death is always an interruption or threat, never experienced as an event. Husserl warns against investing life in "heroic projects" that can't outlast death, suggesting instead activities and values that foster generativity and continuation beyond individual existence.

Derrida: Responsibility, Otherness, and Aporia. Derrida, drawing on phenomenology and ethics, explores death primarily through the lens of responsibility and the encounter with the "Other". Influenced by Levinas, in his book, The Gift of Death, Derrida explores the paradoxes and aporias involved: the impossibility of fully accounting for responsibility either to oneself or to all others. Death, in this reading, exposes the limitations and contradictions inherent in ethical and social norms.

"Surely, there is never anything certain, except death." This maxim or principle has universal validity, since, regardless of culture or age, in principle no one can logically deny it. There are, however, great differences from the perspective of age. Young people generally do not have a possible death in mind, since they see it as distant and rarely consider it seriously. In addition to age, depending on physical conditions, individuals face the issue differently, especially those who face a terminal illness. There are those who face death voluntarily, particularly in countries that legalize euthanasia, which, without being suicide in the strict sense, is a form of taking one's life for the most different reasons. Young Werther, the central character of Goethe's famous novel, commits suicide because it is the only solution to end the torture of not being reciprocated by Charlotte, his beloved, who rejects him.

The theme is repeated in famous novels, particularly *Madame Bovary* by Gustave Flaubert, whose desperate protagonist takes her life by ingesting arsenic.

The famous Stoic philosopher and Roman playwright Lucius Seneca in 65 AD follows the fate of Aristotle by being condemned to death. Seneca, following the tradition at that time of dying by cutting the veins and bleeding slowly to death, a cruel death that allows him to confirm one of the principles of his philosophical writings of seeing death as liberation.

Seneca in his *Letters to Lucilius* or *Moral Epistles to Lucilius* (Epistulae Morales ad Lucilium) written at the end of his life contains a series of wise advice and relevant reflections that serve as inspiration for Michel de Montaigne's *Essays*.

In letter number 19 of the cited work, Seneca clearly distinguishes the need to face at a certain age the inevitable dilemma of confronting death and writes: "Old age is upon us: it is time to begin to pack our luggage. Surely no one can oppose that. We have lived at sea; let us die in port."

Michel de Montaigne, the famous French philosopher of the 16th century, compiled his ideas, philosophy, and work in his *Essays*, which serve as a broad reflection of his experiences and in which he shows himself an admirer of classical writers, among them Seneca himself, Virgil, Cicero, and Plutarch. Like the typical Renaissance scholar, he reads them assiduously seeking inspiration. To understand Montaigne's character and his ideas about the finiteness of life, it is worth reading the

Latin inscription painted on the wall of his rich library:

> «*In the year of Christ 1571, at the age of thirty-eight, on the last day of February, the anniversary of his birth, Michel de Montaigne, long tired of the servitude of the court and public employment, while still whole, retired to the bosom of the virgins* [the Muses], *where in calm and freedom from all worries he would spend what little remains of his life, now more than half exhausted. If fate permits it, he will complete this dwelling, this sweet ancestral retreat; and he has consecrated it to his freedom, tranquility, and leisure.*»

The *Essays* include references to the most diverse topics, from love, friendship, morality, and naturally death, which he alludes to in multiple and varied contexts, having been a very young witness to the death of his very close friend Étienne de La Boétie, of whom he was the translator of his theological works and political manuscripts that Montaigne inherits. The *Essays* are characterized by their conversational tone, their broad scope, and their deep insight into human nature.

It is not surprising that as a Stoic, Baruch Spinoza, one of the greatest classical philosophers, is also considered a follower of Seneca. In his *Ethics*, his main work, pragmatism dominates, especially when he calls for learning to tolerate with tranquility the events that occur during life, including death itself, which "should not worry the free person," since "the power we have could not have extended to the point where we could have avoided those things, since we are part of nature, whose order we follow." (IV, Appendix)

Inspired by Spinoza and classical thinkers, as well as Buddhism and Taoism, Arthur Schopenhauer (1788–1860) becomes one of the most influential philosophers of the 19th century, whose works and ideas were followed by other important thinkers, particularly Nietzsche, who considered himself to be Schopenhauer's successor. His work also influenced Sigmund Freud's ideas about psychoanalysis. The concept of death plays a relevant role in the philosopher's work, since his father, Heinrich Schopenhauer, a successful merchant, committed suicide when his son Arthur was only seventeen years old.

In chapter V, "*The Stages of Life*" in his *Essays, Counsels, and Maxims*, Schopenhauer emphasizes how at the beginning of life we expect a long future, and toward the end we look back and see an extensive past. In this way, the philosopher considers that each period of life has a different color. In childhood, he tells us, "we are more given to using our intellect and less the will," and after that golden age or magical years of learning about the external world, "comes the great period of disillusionment, a period of gradual decay in which all false illusions have been overcome." With great simplicity and eloquence, he considers that the joy and vivacity of youth are due in part to the fact that, when one is climbing the hill of life, "death is not visible," but once one reaches the summit, it is possible to glimpse "death, which, until then, was only known to us by rumors."

In this journey, Schopenhauer considers "that only the old man who sees the entire life and knows its natural course; . . . not only with its beginning, like the rest of humanity, but also with its exit."

In literature, theater, and cinema there are numerous examples of relevant works in which death is a central theme. In Shakespeare's works it is recurrent, as it is in those of his contemporaries Christopher Marlowe and Ben Jonson, who wrote violent scenes. On the "*Not Sweet Shakespeare*" webpage, the number and form of how the celebrated playwright stages death are listed in some detail. It notes that his works contain more than twenty suicides and almost half of the characters die stabbed, beheaded, or poisoned. "Several characters die of shame and quite a few are hanged. Some die of grief and others of insomnia. One is torn apart by a mob, one eaten by a bear, one baked in a pie, one is bitten by a snake, and there is even someone who dies of indigestion."

In *Hamlet*, Shakespeare summarizes the notion of death when the King asks where Polonius's body is located, the faithful advisor to the Kingdom accidentally killed by Hamlet, who responds, "he is among the dust, of which he is a close relative."

Since Hitler came to power, news of suicides has been frequent, first in Germany, mainly among Jews, who, knowing the fate that awaited them in concentration camps, preferred to die in peace and avoid suffering. Later, this phenomenon affected thousands of refugees in France, who from 1938 faced arrests and expulsions, and thus, the desperation of not finding safe places to emigrate.

There are numerous examples of indirect suicides or the desire to die without making it explicit. A relevant example is that of Simone Weil, who from childhood suffered from severe headaches that prevented her from leading a normal life. The writings of the famous French philosopher focus on the notion of human suffering and perhaps anticipating the form of her own death, "Weil was beginning to know the immense horror of the so-called Holodomor—extermination by hunger—of the years 1932 and 1933 when four million Ukrainians suffered a horrific death by starvation that Stalin's administration had deliberately provoked." Paradoxically, according to the medical certificate, Weil died on August 24, 1943, in a sanatorium in England caused by "cardiac insufficiency [...] resulting from starvation and tuberculosis," particularly because "the deceased refused to eat." Richard Rees, one of Weil's biographers, presents several possible hypotheses to understand her death, particularly "her compassion for the suffering of her compatriots in occupied France and her love and close imitation of Christ."

Another example is Walter Benjamin, the celebrated philosopher and critic of mass media, who faces death debating about a life that with Hitler's rise to power loses all his rights due to his Jewish origin, which forces him to leave Germany to become a refugee.

Benjamin, like thousands of people of the most diverse origins fleeing from the horrors committed by the Nazis, takes refuge in France. In July 1940, France approves a decree by which it suspends the right of asylum and establishes the government's obligation to extradite Jewish refugees. With this, France ceased to be a safe place, and thus, Benjamin had little time to leave that country before mass deportations began.

The circumstances and deterioration of the refugee condition make suicide an option for Benjamin. In his book *The Fire of Freedom*, Wolfram Eilenberger describes Hannah Arendt's encounter with Benjamin in Marseille, where he had all the necessary documents to emigrate to the United States, including a passage from Lisbon to New York. However, he does not have the exit visa that France stopped issuing, which forced Benjamin and many others to undertake the hazardous journey through the Pyrenees to reach Spain, where he receives the news that he will not be able to continue with his plans and that he would be deported back to France. Unable to face adversity, Benjamin committed suicide with an overdose of morphine tablets. The official record of the city of Portbou registers September 26, 1940, as the date of death. Benjamin's colleague, Arthur Koestler, who also fled from France and attempted suicide by taking some of the morphine tablets, survived.

Following the chain of suicides of German intellectuals, like Walter Benjamin and dozens of writers, the biographer and novelist Stefan Zweig, a refugee in Brazil, desperate about his precarious situation and an uncertain future, dies along with his wife Lotte from an overdose of barbiturates that they ingest in their house in Petrópolis, Brazil, on February 23, 1942, eight years after leaving his country following the rise of the Nazi Party in Germany, to emigrate to England, later to New York, and finally to Brazil where he takes his life.

As its title indicates, Leo Tolstoy's famous novel *The Death of Ivan Ilyich*, published in 1886, describes the conversations of Ivan's colleagues upon reading in the press the news of the death of their bench companion at the court, after a long and painful illness. Knowing the weaknesses of human nature, Tolstoy describes the reactions of those present in the court office, particularly what that death could bring about in terms of changes or promotions among them or their acquaintances.

"Now, surely, I will get Shtabel's or Vinnikov's position," Fyodor Vasilyevich said to himself. "They have promised it to me for a long time; and the promotion will mean a salary increase of eight hundred rubles, not counting the bonus."

The novel refers to the scenes and conversations of the deceased's relatives at the wake, as well as the concern of Ivan's wife, who despite being clear about what "could be extracted from the treasury as a result of that death; wanted to know if more could be extracted."

The novel recounts the eventful life of Ivan, a successful judicial career that ends after a long suffering that his doctor for a long time avoided answering the question of whether his illness was serious or not.

Another extraordinary novel in which the theme of death is also included in the title is *Death in Venice* by Nobel Prize in Literature winner Thomas Mann. Published in 1912 and brought to film in a spectacular realization by Luchino Visconti. It deals with the infatuation suffered by Gustav von Aschenbach, a distinguished mature German writer, during a summer in an elegant hotel on the Venice Lido. An infatuation produced by a Polish adolescent named Tadzio, endowed with extraordinary beauty according to the author's description. With the departure of Tadzio and his family, terrified by an imminent cholera epidemic that the authorities hide to avoid the exodus of tourists, Von Aschenbach decides to stay in Venice and face the certain death that the disease anticipated.

Thomas Mann also approaches death from the perspective of anticipated death in his extraordinary novel *Doctor Faustus*, published in 1947. The central character, Adrian Leverkühn, deliberately contracts syphilis so that through madness he can incite his creativity and produce an innovative and revolutionary concert. Adrian makes a pact with the demon so that he can live the necessary time to complete that work that he titles "Apocalypse" and subsequently composes a second oratorio, "The Lamentation of Doctor Faustus." The composer, in addition to suffering terrible headaches produced by the disease and tragic deaths of loved ones caused by having broken his pact with Lucifer.

Jacques Derrida, the French philosopher famous for his theory of deconstruction, in an interview conducted by Jean Birnbaum, originally published in *Le Monde*, under the title *Learn to live at last*. Derrida takes the traditional philosophical maxim, attributed to Plato and collected by Montaigne, according to which philosophizing is learning to die. A few months before his anticipated death resulting from a serious cancer, Derrida confessed: "I remain uneducable when it comes to any kind of wisdom about knowing how to die or, if you prefer, knowing how to live. I still have not learned or picked up anything on this subject. The time of the reprieve is rapidly running out."

Finally, to end the arbitrary and disordered account of quotes from authors and books that face and describe the phenomenon of death, there is the novel by Dr. Irvin D. Yalom, a well-known psychotherapist and author of novels, who chooses Schopenhauer as the central character of one of his books: *The Schopenhauer Cure*. Like his other two novels based on prominent philosophers, Nietzsche and Spinoza (*When Nietzsche Wept* and *The Spinoza Problem*), Yalom, in addition to using fictional situations, inserts important information about these three thinkers in each of his novels, including quotes and historical facts about the time they lived and relevant biographical information. Along with this type of objective information, the biographical novels are full of situations created by the author, including dialogues, some based on letters, biographies, or anecdotal information. These famous novels have the advantage of making the ideas of these great, highly individualistic philosophers accessible to the general public.

Yalom's *The Schopenhauer Cure* is directly related to Arthur Schopenhauer's *The Stages of Life*, mentioned earlier. In Yalom's novel *Julius*, a successful

psychotherapist is diagnosed with malignant mela-
noma after a routine medical examination. Julius's
doctor, when communicating this unexpected and
tragic news to his patient, tells him that he will
only have one year of healthy life, after which his
health will begin to deteriorate rapidly, and he will
finally die.

Devastated by the news, Julius struggles to find
a meaningful way to make use of the limited time
he has left to live. He decides to continue with
his professional practice and meet regularly with
the therapy group he leads. Also, he wants to see
how effective his practice was in curing his patients. Reviewing the files of former patients, he
finds Phillip, who twenty years earlier was an un-
repentant sexual predator with an incurable sexual
addiction that turned his life into a constant search
for personal satisfaction, which implied a source of
pain for dozens of female victims.

Julius finds Phillip, who now has a doctor-
ate in philosophy and has become an expert on
Schopenhauer. Following the teachings and lifestyle
of the philosopher, Phillip finds a "cure" and a
substitution for his previous destructive behavior.
Phillip considers Schopenhauer as the therapist
who "made me aware that we are condemned to
turn ceaselessly in the wheel of will: we desire something, we acquire it, we enjoy a brief moment of
satisfaction, which quickly fades into boredom . . ."

The relationship between a terminally ill therapist and a former patient, now a philosopher, serves
as a compelling metaphor to illustrate the process of
confronting and coping with an impending death.

V. The Terrorist

Machiavelli: Terror, Statecraft, and Power. Machiavelli believed cruelty, fraud, and conspiracy were essential tools for political ends. He considered them political virtues when used to establish or protect state order. He stressed the need for rulers to inspire fear without hatred and supported pragmatic, adaptable measures against threats like terrorism to maintain stability and power.

Francis Fukuyama: Globalization and Modern Terrorism. Francis Fukuyama argued that events like September 11 didn't fundamentally overturn his "end of history" thesis. He believed terrorist groups oppose liberal democracy, not new systems. He saw terrorism as rational political violence advancing ideological causes, often due to states' failure to address social, economic, or identity grievances. Fukuyama emphasized that global fragmentation and radicalization challenge traditional state structures, requiring nuanced responses to social insecurity and identity struggles exploited by terrorist groups.

Henry Kissinger: Terrorism, Realism, and World Order. Henry Kissinger applied a realist perspective to terrorism, emphasizing that no superpower can maintain world order alone. He advocated for multilateral and realist approaches, criticizing unilateral responses and urging cooperation and democracy to counter extremist violence. Kissinger viewed terrorism as a threat to state legitimacy and stability, advocating for swift defeat to prevent emboldening anti-state movements. He argued that terrorism fostered ideological and cultural conflicts, especially between the West and militant Islam, requiring strategic engagement to halt empire-building and terrorist expansion.

Joseph Conrad is considered one of the most important writers of the 20th century. He was born in 1857 in Berdichev, a region of Poland that today belongs to Ukraine. He became a British citizen at the age of 29, using English as a novelist and writer of dozens of short stories, novels, and travel journals, mainly in the African colonies. He is less known for his prophetic novels about political intrigues and conflicts in Europe that reveal his profound knowledge and vision of these complicated subjects.

The two Joseph Conrad novels discussed below are diabolical portraits of terrorism whose characters, situations, and conversations could well seem extracted from current events. The characters in both novels are people dealing with isolation, loneliness, hesitation, and largely the inability to interpret the world around them with realism, confidence, or security.

In his political novels, *The Secret Agent* and *Under Western Eyes*, situations are presented that can easily be identified with the real world. Although these extraordinary novels are fictional, both contain rich descriptions of certain plots or terrorist activities, of "agent provocateurs" and spies paid by foreign governments.

The Secret Agent, written in 1907, is the story of Mr. Verloc, an agent paid by the French Government to report on the activities and plans of socialists, anarchists, and other clandestine political figures living in London. These types of personalities would meet late at night in Mr. Verloc's small shop which, on the surface, sells "obscure newspapers, badly printed, with titles like 'The Torch', 'The Gong', flashy titles in the window that display photographs of more or less naked dancers." Mr. Verloc is also one of the vice-presidents of an organization called "The Future of the Proletariat."

The main objective of hiring this type of agent is to warn the governments that recruit them about the potentially dangerous activities of radical groups. Additionally, governments that pay for this type of "dark agent" also try to increase their influence in other countries.

Despite these connections, Mr. Verloc enjoys a comfortable bourgeois double life with his family until he receives a "peremptory letter" summoning him to the French Embassy during the day and not at odd hours as in the past, an unprecedented and unpleasant situation that could damage his image with his comrades.

Verloc is received with some contempt at the French Embassy by a new First Secretary, who says, "I have here some of your reports" using a mocking tone, calling Verloc's reports useless and expensive. "In the time of Baron Stott-Wartenheim (the former French ambassador), we had many weak people running this embassy." And he continues: "What is required nowadays is not writing . . . now we want facts . . ."

To convey what he means by "facts" and what Mr. Verloc is obliged to do to continue receiving payment, the French diplomat explains that his government considers it "dangerous" that England has an absurd "sentimental reluctance for the position of individual freedom" in opposition to harsher measures to combat political dissidents, which will soon be discussed at an international meeting on security issues. "What we want is to administer a tonic to the Milan Conference," and he says, ". . . their deliberations on international action for the repression of political crimes don't seem to get anywhere. England is falling behind," states the bureaucrat.

The First Secretary continues his monologue outlining his plan to "induce" England to accept new repressive policies. He orders Mr. Verloc to organize a series of terrorist acts to be "executed here in this country; not just planned here." This will surprise and frighten the middle class, inducing them to favor radical measures so they feel safe. These acts, he says ". . . must be sufficiently surprising, effective. Let them be directed against buildings . . . the fetish of the hour that all the bourgeoisie recognizes . . ."

Almost like an ominous anticipated warning, 94 years after this novel was published, the United States suffered a series of well-planned terrorist attacks in 2001, mainly directed at buildings, killing more than 3,000 people and destroying the Twin

Towers of the World Trade Center, which was one of the most admired Manhattan landmarks.

In this classic novel, Joseph Conrad demonstrates his profound understanding of the radical minds of his time behind the convulsive political intrigues that created serious tensions and conflicts, which ended with World War I. It is clear that Conrad was aware of the destructive nature of radical ideologies that tended to justify violence and terrorism, disregarding innocent human lives for a supposed good of an abstract cause.

Under Western Eyes is another important Conrad novel on the same subject but with a different approach. First published in 1911, it deals with the dark human aspects linked to extreme ideologies.

As mentioned before, in *The Secret Agent*, Conrad describes what he calls the "dark heart" of the First Secretary of the French Embassy in London, who unscrupulously is ready to destroy a historic building and, if necessary, kill innocent people in order to force the British to adopt repressive measures against their political dissidents.

In this second novel, Conrad chooses an individual, willing to carry out a terrorist act, as another example of the "dark heart." Haldin, one of the main characters in this extraordinary novel, is a young Russian student who proudly identifies himself as a "destroyer," after murdering the hated repressive official Mr. P, and possibly innocent passersby, by throwing a bomb in a street.

After the successful terrorist act, Haldin hides in the house of Razumov, a solitary student he knows at the university who immediately feels that his future is threatened by Haldin's ominous presence in his student room. Haldin says: "It was I who eliminated P this morning," trying to make his situation clear, and continues in a defiant tone: "Men like me are necessary to make room for autonomous and thinking men like you," degrading his colleague, who now becomes an involuntary accomplice. "All I want you to do is help me disappear." With these words, Haldin begins to set the stage for a series of events that radically changed Razumov's life, as he reveals in his diary ". . . I, who love my country, since I have nothing else to love and to put my faith in, should I continue to have faith in my future, now ruined by this bloodthirsty fanatic?"

From here, the story develops with a series of unexpected events, showing Conrad's unique talent as a storyteller who describes in great detail the ominous symptoms of the era in Russia before the 1917 revolution. The story contains quotes from Razumov's diary that he begins after his encounter with the terrorist. In it, he writes about his internal conflicts, his family background, and the painful path of awakening that connects him with extremists and revolutionaries, as well as with rich and powerful individuals both in Russia and in the West.

The plot uses Razumov's internal tribulations, in addition to his diary and the conversations that take place in Geneva about the future Russian revolution that is brewing and the Western world's inability to understand it. To delve deeper into the subject, Conrad uses in the novel a Russian emigrant in Geneva, who tries to explain to her English professor what that revolution means: "You think it's a class conflict, or a conflict of interests, since social movements are in Europe, but in Russia it's different." The professor, who seems to be Conrad's own voice, when responding to his Russian interlocutor: "A violent revolution falls into the hands of narrow-minded fanatics and tyrannical hypocrites at the beginning." The professor goes further in his negative views on revolutions: "The scrupulous and the just, the noble, human, and devoted natures; the disinterested and intelligent may start a movement, but it moves away from them. They are not the leaders of a revolution. They are its victims: the victims of disgust, disenchantment, often of remorse." Clearly, here Conrad anticipates with great lucidity the future of the Soviet Revolution five years later. In reality, his comments remain valid.

Among other characters living in Geneva, *Under Western Eyes* also includes an influential Russian writer who advocates radical feminist ideas, and Madame de S, a wealthy woman with an aristocratic family background, famous for hosting "soirées" in her castle with Russians and political conspirators. The character of Madame de S seems to have been inspired by Madame de Staël, the 19th-century French political writer, who also lived near Geneva in a castle and was famous for her "salon"-style gatherings, attended by refugees and political thinkers in the Napoleonic era.

This novel, written at the dawn of World War I, in which millions of people lost their lives, was triggered by the assassination (by a terrorist) of

Austrian Archduke Franz Ferdinand and his wife in Sarajevo on June 28, 1914, three years after *Under Western Eyes* was published.

These similarities, which could be considered premonitions, were repeated again 90 years later with the assassination of John F. Kennedy in Dallas in 1963. Additionally, as we noted, terrorist acts targeting the Twin Towers in New York on September 11, 2001, are added, as in the aforementioned novel.

Reading *Under Western Eyes* and *The Secret Agent* presents with great clarity the personality or character of the terrorist and certainly helps to better understand what Joseph Conrad meant by the title of his famous novel *Heart of Darkness*.

Conrad's novels are not the only classic novels that deal with these complex current political and social themes; Fyodor Dostoevsky, about 30 years before Conrad, wrote *The Possessed* (also known as *Demons* or *The Devils*), which also addresses terrorism, a theme that unfortunately remains very much alive today.

The famous English scholar and writer Aileen Kelly, in her introduction to the book of essays by philosopher Isaiah Berlin, *Russian Thinkers*, highlights Dostoevsky's aforementioned novel and says: "In an attempt to explain the Bolshevik movement in Russia before 1917 to Lady Ottoline Morrell, Bertrand Russell commented that, however appalling the type of government most suitable for Russia seemed: 'you will understand it better if you ask yourself how Dostoevsky's characters should be governed.'"

In *The Possessed*, the character of the radical Russian intellectual class is presented, along with the personality and ideas of its leaders, who, as the novel describes, are a small group of the most diverse social origin but united by a sense of mission that equates to that of a religious sect for their fanatical devotion to the task of destroying the existing order. Nikolai Stavrogin, the central character, is a master of conspiracy, exercises extraordinary influence over the other characters, whom he dominates and condemns to face the consequences.

Written in first person with a narrator who describes the complicated chain of social events, romances, duels, suicides, murders and the events that follow the arrest of those responsible for an terrorist plot is loosely inspired by real-life events, particularly the murder of a Moscow student by a group of radical revolutionaries. Often regarded as one of Dostoyevsky's most scathing critique of nihilism and radical political ideologies, *The Possessed* delves into the chaos and moral decay that result from embracing extreme beliefs. The novel vividly illustrates the devastating consequences of ideological extremism, which can lead to societal disruption and personal ruin.

The novel is inspired by real events and its characters according to various studies are very similar to members of the aristocracy, and Russian exiles that Conrad portrays with great talent in his aforementioned novels.

VI. Wealth, Influence, and Fame

Montaigne, Schopenhauer, and Nietzsche each present distinctive—often critical—perspectives on wealth, influence, and fame, viewing them neither as sources of true happiness nor as ultimate goods. Their reflections share a skepticism about social standing and external validation, emphasizing instead personal cultivation, authenticity, and inner values.

Montaigne, despite his wealth and privilege, viewed fame and fortune as problematic, leading to superficiality, vanity, and dependence on others' opinions. He believed human suffering arises from living "by reference to others," prioritizing public opinion over reality. Montaigne warned that excessive concern for riches is avarice, and wealth's value lies in purpose, not accumulation or appearance. He considered fame an unstable foundation for happiness and fortune a powerful determinant limiting human agency and making worldly achievements unreliable.

Nietzsche was deeply critical of conventional ambitions toward money, influence, and fame. He maintained that only those with true "spirit" or creative power should have wealth; otherwise, riches merely lead to social danger, boredom, and further spiritual impoverishment. Nietzsche critiqued the pursuit of money as a lesser, even ignoble, form of power, emphasizing the superiority of intellectual and creative pursuits. He saw fame and influence as masking deeper dependency and mediocrity, fueling a herd mentality and envy among the masses. True nobility, for Nietzsche, comes from self-overcoming, artistic or philosophical achievement, and the courage to create values beyond conformity and social validation.

Anthony Trollope's *The Way We Live Now* delivers a biting, satirical critique of Victorian society's relentless pursuit of money, power, and social status. At the heart of the narrative is Augustus Melmotte, a charismatic yet unscrupulous financier whose meteoric rise and dramatic fall serve as a microcosm of the era's moral decay. Trollope masterfully interweaves the destinies of numerous characters, each representing a different facet of Victorian life, to expose the profound social and ethical ramifications of a world increasingly dominated by financial speculation and the commodification of reputation.

Melmotte's lavish lifestyle captivates London society, blinding many to the fraudulent nature of his enterprises. Through characters, Trollope explores how fortune-hunting and idealistic but naive individuals navigate a society where appearances often trump integrity. The novel delves into the corrosive effects of greed, the superficiality of social climbing, and the vulnerability of traditional values in the face of rampant materialism. Furthermore, Trollope examines the role of the press in shaping public opinion and the ease with which reputations can be manufactured and destroyed. *The Way We Live Now* transcends a mere narrative of financial impropriety, evolving into a sharp critique of the ethical concessions and systemic maladies that render its characters and scenarios eerily resonant with our own era. The novel masterfully dissects the corrosive influence of greed, ambition, and social climbing, mirroring the contemporary obsession with wealth and status. The parallels are striking: the speculative bubbles and fraudulent schemes of the novel find their echoes in modern-day economic crises, while the characters' willingness to sacrifice integrity for social advancement and money reflects the pervasive pressure to succeed at any cost.

In *The Great Gatsby*, F. Scott Fitzgerald masterfully portrays money as a corrupting force, showing how it distorts the moral compass of individuals. Jay Gatsby's pursuit of wealth to win back Daisy leads to his downfall, while Tom Buchanan embodies the callousness of inherited wealth. The novel explores how both "old money" and "new money" contribute to moral decay, revealing the destructive nature of wealth.

William Shakespeare's *King Lear* presents another stark depiction of how wealth and power erode familial bonds and incite madness. Lear's rash decision to divide his kingdom based on flattery unleashes a chain of events fueled by greed and ambition. His daughters, Goneril and Regan, initially feign affection to secure their inheritance, but quickly reveal their greed and cruelty. In sharp contrast with her sisters, Cordelia refuses to participate in this performance of false affection. She simply declares that she loves her father "according to my bond; no more nor less," refusing to compromise her integrity for material gain, choosing exile over false flattery. Once Goneril and Regan get their inheritance, they start treating their father with "callousness and cruelty" and ultimately casting the King out without his wealth, army, and status. Lear's descent into madness underscores the destructive consequences of prioritizing material wealth over genuine human connection. Cordelia remains loyal to her father, eventually returning with an army to restore him to his rightful place. The play serves as a potent reminder that true riches lie not in possessions, but in love, loyalty, and integrity, qualities often sacrificed in the ruthless pursuit of power and wealth.

VII. Friends

*I need no friend who changes when I change
and who nods when I nod; my shadow does it
much better.*

—Plutarch

Friendship and the character of the friend is perhaps one of the most difficult to define due to the multiple associations and the superficial character with which it is regularly used. Plutarch in a brief phrase defines friendship for convenience, which is common in politics and business, particularly linking friendship to a high public position, where friendship is related to whoever temporarily holds a position and not with the individual when they no longer hold it.

Correspondence between two individuals is a way to find long-term relationships that could be defined as lasting friendships that share identity of values and interests, independent of present situations.

Books with collections of letters written by prominent artists, writers, thinkers, politicians, psychotherapists, etc. are rich sources of knowledge that help us understand different aspects of human nature, such as friendship, love, etc.

This literary genre allows readers to explore various facets of personality and temperament, especially of those who disguised their true nature or were distorted in their biographies, which are sometimes full of lies and flattery.

Most published letters contain personal exchanges between people who devoted time and passion to correspondence with their lovers, families, friends, etc. Such material reveals the character, mood, taste, and personal challenges of the letter writers. It also gives us the opportunity to know the atmosphere of the time in which they were written and, in some cases, what was happening when they were written or the spirit of their time or *Zeitgeist*.

In general, published correspondences were maintained and organized by the writers and/or their recipients, and after their death, in many cases these writings were transmitted to their relatives or friends, which sometimes resulted in them ending up in museums, foundations, or private collections. These institutions or people who are in possession of the collections sometimes license the rights to publish books with selections made by experts or close relatives of the authors, who sometimes provide the context of the letters.

Correspondence also serves as an important source of information for biographers who can quote the biographers directly, using their own voices and intimate feelings that are always relevant for readers to understand the character. For example, the controversial prolific Russian author Lou Andreas-Salomé used letters to support biographies about the life and works of Friedrich Nietzsche and poet Rainer Maria Rilke, respectively, both romantically linked to her during their lives.

There are also many examples of fictional letters that are regularly used in novels as part of a plot, including Irving Yalom's novel *When Nietzsche Wept* in which letters from this famous philosopher are used to construct a fictional story based on real-life events.

We find multiple examples of films in which letters play a central role in the story. One example is *The Go Between* (1970) by Joseph Losey, where in the summer of 1900, a 13-year-old boy helped carry letters between two secret lovers. The film is based on a novel by L. P. Hartley with the same title.

Another example of books containing letters is *Vita and Virginia* by Eileen Atkins, which is largely based on the intelligent and passionate letters between the two famous British writers; Vita Sackville-West and Virginia Woolf who exchanged letters for about 20 years until Virginia Woolf's suicide in 1941.

Among the collections of letters published in book form, mainly by people who lived between the late 19th century and the first half of the 20th century, a turbulent era with two devastating world wars, but at the same time full of creativity and romanticism during which heartfelt friendships were forged. I find particularly important for understanding historical contexts and literary backgrounds the correspondence between Thomas Mann and Hermann Hesse, the two recognized Nobel Prize winners in literature. In their letters, it is possible to distinguish the anxiety and fear that the rise of Nazism in Germany and Hitler's rise to power produced in them.

Both wrote about the impact that this criminal regime had on their lives and their literary works, as well as their feelings when witnessing the tragedy through which Germany, their country, went during those years. Even from Hitler's early days in power, both authors anticipated that something terrible was happening in their country. As Thomas Mann mentioned to Hesse in a letter from July 1933, "The day-to-day news from Germany, the deception, the violence, the ridiculous spectacle of 'historical greatness,' the pure cruelty, fill me with horror, contempt, and disgust." In 1934, Mann wrote: "I am so distressed by the events in Germany, which are a torment to my moral and critical conscience, which has prevented me from continuing with my current literary work." Hesse, on the other hand, expressed his fear for the safety of his family and close friends: "At this moment, it is likely that any anger aroused by my name will bring physical mistreatment and other problems to my friends," he wrote in February 1937.

In addition to these comments charged with fear and resentment, in most of their letters, references are made to the books they were reading and those they were writing at the time. With great eloquence, Pete Hamill wrote an introduction to the latest English reprint (the edition which my company published), describing his experience reading the letters, ". . . I feel like a privileged guest in a special room, sitting in front of a fireplace somewhere keeping silent, listening to these men talk."

To complement the opinions of these two exceptional writers regarding the horrors that followed Hitler's destructive path from the early 1930s, there are also some relevant passages in the letter that Winston Churchill wrote to his wife Clementine before the United Kingdom's participation in World War II, giving his vision of the events that had led to declaring a state of war. These personal letters provide a spontaneous personal description of the challenges his country and Europe faced at that time.

On a less somber subject, I find refreshing the letters from Rainer Maria Rilke to Lou Andreas-Salomé, under the title *Rilke and Andreas-Salomé: a love story in letters* and his own *Letters to a Young Poet*, which include references to poetry and love. The content of these letters shows his frankness and desire to have intellectual conversations using that indirect route. The letters are full of wisdom, showing at the same time the passionate sensitivity, unique to this great artist, as well as his immense capacity to express and discuss love and friendship.

The same characteristic can also be found in Franz Kafka's letters to his two lovers, Milena and Felice, to whom he wrote almost daily. From the two collections, we realize that Kafka is not only a great novelist, but also a fertile and passionate correspondent.

The collections of letters from avant-garde artist Van Gogh to Theo, his brother, are full of references to what art and painting meant to him, as well as to other famous artists like Monet and Gauguin with whom the Dutch artist had a close relationship.

Sigmund Freud's extensive correspondence with his fiancée, colleagues, patients, friends, and family shows how the father of psychoanalysis used letters to share his knowledge and vision about the human condition beyond his professional sphere.

Sending letters in the past required time and patience. Correspondence has its own protocol: once a letter is completed, it is usually sent folded in an envelope and, in some cases, sealed with wax to ensure its integrity and privacy. Some wealthy people and government officials in the past had trusted messengers; others might ask friends or family members to deliver their letters just to feel more secure. Postal services have existed since antiquity in a relay manner similar to ours, with one messenger passing letters to another at a certain post or tavern along defined routes that connected different cities and even countries. With the introduction of a more affordable national postal service along with an increasingly educated and traveled middle class, by the mid-18th century, letter writing began to flourish with messages exchanged almost worldwide. These forms of communication require people to wait patiently for weeks before messengers and subsequently mail carriers bring responses to their messages. To illustrate what it meant to wait for a letter, I quote the last paragraph of one of Mrs. Churchill's letters to her husband Winston in 1915: "My answer will be ready here in a few minutes and I eagerly await a letter from you." Another example is that of Freud frustrated with the slow postal system expressed in a letter to his colleague Carl Jung in 1911: "I am writing to you again this year, because I cannot always wait for you to respond and I prefer to write when I have time and am in the mood . . ."

An interesting phenomenon of letter communication is the fact that writers active in this type of exchange with their colleagues, lovers, or friends, in general, are disciplined as they tend to keep collections organized perhaps thinking that their correspondence will be of interest to their families or will be a reference when published in book form after they die. In some cases, a close family member becomes the editor, as is the case with *The Personal Letters of the Churchills*, whose selection and editing was handled by their daughter Mary Soames.

Similarly, it was Freud's son, Ernest L., who compiled and edited a selection of his father's more than 350 letters addressed to Einstein, Thomas Mann, H. G. Wells, Maria Montessori, Carl Jung, Romain Rolland, and many others, under the title *The Letters of Sigmund Freud*. Showing Freud's rich correspondence culture, we find two collections: *The Letters of Sigmund Freud & Otto Rank* and *Freud To Wilhelm Fliess (1887–1904)*. These letters provide invaluable insights into the origins of psychoanalysis, Sigmund Freud's personality, his inner world, relationships, intellectual interests, and the historical backdrop of his life and work, offering a unique perspective on this influential thinker.

Most editions of letter collections in book form are made by academics who are given access to the archives of the original copies. These authors or editors require not only a deep understanding of the historical context but also an eye for detail to be able to decide which letters to include and which to omit, always balancing the desire for completeness with the need for readability and coherence.

Reading these collections gives an idea of the richness of the form of written communication that is gradually losing ground with the advent of modern technology, including personal computers, the Internet, and portable electronic devices like iPhones and iPads, along with many social platforms that have changed the way we read, interact, and communicate with others.

The new media for communication show a striking contrast through a simpler and instantaneous process: messages can be sent shortly after finishing with the click of a button. Particularly with improved email or message applications on smartphones, correspondences tend to be fast, even instantaneous. Computers, smartphones, and tablets have replaced ink, paper, and typewriters, while the Internet and wireless communications have greatly diminished the role and importance of traditional slower postal services.

Today, almost everyone is connected, receiving and sending dozens of text messages, emails a day, and probably posting notes and photos on Twitter, Facebook, and other social platforms. The new communication styles are radically different from those of traditional letter writing, especially because letters are generally written and read in an intimate, reserved, and private manner.

Today, people collect "friends" and "likes" when, in reality, in most cases, they are acquaintances or shared a school, a club, or an activity in the past.

The abandonment of physical letter writing as a communication method, replaced by email, is unprecedented, as Malcolm Jones, the well-known book review author, considers that the "decline in letter writing constitutes such a vast cultural change that in the future, historians may divide time not between B.C. and A.D., but between the epochs when people wrote letters and when they stopped doing so."

Friendship is demonstrated in various ways, regardless of long-distance communication. There are a large number of novels that describe friendships and intimate relationships of all kinds. Among the novels that describe close friendships, *Tonio Kröger* by Thomas Mann and *Narcissus and Goldmund* by Hermann Hesse stand out. The first, published in 1903, describes an intense relationship between two young men with a few years' difference but with different education and personality. Hans and Tonio, the two central characters of Mann's novel, in their youth begin a complex relationship full of nuances, which begins with the walk home after school, during which the young men embark on serious conversations. Their parents were men with important status in their city. Hans's family had been owners for several generations of lumber companies; while Tonio was the son of Consul Kröger, a grain merchant, and his residence was the largest and best situated in the entire city. Tonio writes in his diary the infatuation he suffers for his friend and the experiences that lead him to be an artist and writer and to a bohemian life that allows him to intellectualize his feelings, maturing the experiences of a very close youth friendship.

In Hermann Hesse's novel published in 1930, Narcissus is a talented teacher in a cloister school and is destined for religious and intellectual life. Goldmund, on the contrary, after a sexual experience with a gypsy, discovers that he has no vocation to be a monk and, helped by Narcissus, leaves the cloister to wander the world and lead a life full of love adventures that almost cost him his life. Thanks to a fortuitous encounter with his youth friend, who saves him from being executed and thus recovering their friendship, the two reflect on the different paths their contrasting lives have taken.

Jorge Luis Borges addresses the theme of friendship recurrently in his work, in some cases contrasting it with love. In the book that contains several interviews that, at eighty years old, he had with Willis Barnstone, Alastair Reid, John Coleman, Jorge Oclander, and several more in Buenos Aires and especially in American universities, Borges presents his ideas eloquently. In his responses, it is possible to find the essence of his thinking on the subject. To the question about what friendship means to him, a question that is repeated throughout the conversations, Borges responds, "I believe that friendship is perhaps the most essential fact of life. Friendship, as Adolfo Bioy Casares said, has an advantage over love, in the sense that it doesn't need proof." In the case of love, you always worry about being loved or not, and you are always in a sad mood, in a state of anxiety, while in friendship, you may not have seen the friend for more than a year; he may even have despised you, may have tried to avoid you, but if you are his friend, and you know that he is your friend, then you don't have to worry about it. Friendship, once established, needs nothing; it simply continues." In Borgesian terms, he considers friendship as something magical and a kind of spell.

A modern vision of the concept is presented in Thomas Bernhard's autobiographical novel, *Wittgenstein's Nephew*, in which the complicated and at the same time problematic relationship with Paul Wittgenstein, the nephew of the author of the famous *Tractatus Logico-philosophicus*, and one of the greatest philosophers of our time, is described in some detail.

The first part of the book recounts the experience of both friends hospitalized in Austria at the same time in a huge and complex hospital in separate pavilions. Bernhard was treated for a lung disease, and Paul Wittgenstein for a mental illness.

In the book, Bernhard presents several examples of the dark image of his friend Paul's health, who from childhood had a predisposition to an illness, which without having been precisely diagnosed, afflicted him all his life, until his death, adding: "In each crisis, the doctors would use the term manic or depressive, and they were always wrong."

The author describes his relationship with Paul, using moments, conversations, and relevant traits, including Paul's problems with his enormously wealthy family.

The book describes Paul's passion for music, especially opera and particularly orchestral works by Mozart and Schumann. Bernhard lists the most important opera houses that Paul visited during his travels to Milan, London, New York, Berlin, which, according to his friend, none was comparable to Vienna.

Bernhard recalls how music lovers considered Paul as one of Vienna's most passionate opera attendees, noting that he was feared on opening nights. As if he was enthusiastic, he would carry the whole house with him by starting to applaud a few seconds before the rest. If, on the other hand, it was not to his taste, he would start whistling, which would make the most expensive productions failures.

Bernhard was also a music lover. His grandfather regularly took him to concerts, including those conducted by Herbert von Karajan in Berlin, whom he admired since childhood. He observed and studied the famous conductor for decades, considering him the most important conductor of the century, along with Carl Schuricht. On the contrary, his friend Paul had a fervent hatred towards Karajan, whom he habitually described as a mere charlatan.

If music was an area that united the two friends, Bernhard highlights where tastes were divergent. For example, he remembers that one of Paul's passions that they did not share was Formula One car races. Coming from a very wealthy family, Paul was a race car driver, counting among his friends several world champions in this field. In the second half of his life, he had to give up racing, as he no longer had the money to sustain that taste and had to adjust to a budget that his relatives granted him.

The book is full of anecdotes from his friend's peculiar life, including the strangest and most eccentric actions like squandering money in luxury restaurants and bars. In this context, Bernhard tells the story of Paul's whims, like a sudden desire to go to Paris taking a taxi in the center of Vienna, with which the driver, who knew him, nevertheless drove him the distance to where a Parisian aunt had to pay the taxi driver for the extravagant trip.

Since the book is written in first person, it gives the reader a unique perspective of Thomas Bernhard's enormous talent and antagonistic personality that produced so many enemies and detractors, which for some analysts was one of the impediments to obtaining a well-deserved Nobel Prize in Literature.

Among the many controversies, Bernhard is associated with his repeated criticisms of Austrian society and explicit disdain for award ceremonies. With humor, he considers those events to be the most intolerable thing in the world. In his own words, they do nothing to improve the writer's position, as he had believed before receiving his first prize, but rather they degrade them in the most embarrassing way. He recognizes only the idea of money associated with prizes allowed him to endure these ceremonies.

Among the vivid anecdotes of his unpleasant experiences receiving public awards was the ceremony at the Academy of Sciences of Austria to receive the prestigious "Grillparzer Literary Prize" commemorating the centenary of the death of the famous Austrian writer. He describes the feeling of frustration he experiences upon arriving at the prestigious institution that morning with his friends and being surprised to see that there was no one there to receive him. "I waited in the lobby for a good quarter of an hour with my friends, but no one recognized me, much less received me, despite the fact that my friends and I spent all the time looking around." Bernhard recounts the details that followed: "The minister had taken her place in the front row in front of the podium. The Vienna Philharmonic was nervously tuning up, and the president of the Academy of Sciences, a man named Hunger, was running anxiously back and forth on the podium, while only my friends and I knew what was delaying the ceremony."

The Chilean novelist, poet, and essayist Roberto Bolaño, in his award-winning novel *The Savage Detectives* ("Mexicans Lost in Mexico"), presents us with another manifestation of a more relaxed friendship and, in a broader sense, the friendship between a group of young university students with common interests corresponding to a generation. The novel is written in diary form, narrating the relationships of the narrator, Juan García Madero, the central character, with his friends, girlfriends, and their families in a complex plot of interactions and situations, as well as the description of the places where the different characters live, the neighborhoods, particularly the Condesa colony, bars, and restaurants of Mexico City, where he lived for several years.

The novel begins with the narrator describing his entry to the Faculty of Law, but in less than a month, he decides to enroll in "Julio César Álamo's poetry workshop" at the Faculty of Philosophy and Letters. Since it is a novel narrated largely in first person, the character introduces his friends who form a group that calls itself "the real visceralists or viscerrealistas and even vicerrealistas as they sometimes like to call themselves." The group's name is inspired by a literary movement of the twenties called visceral realism.

With great detail and a sense of humor, the novel describes the debates in the group and the divisions, jokes, and arguments, even insults and fights with the narrator, creating distances that were later resolved in a friendly manner. As an example of the type of interaction within the group, Bolaño writes: "The closing of the evening was surprising. Álamo challenged Ulises Lima to read one of his poems. He didn't need to be asked twice and took from a jacket pocket some dirty and wrinkled papers. What horror, I thought, this fool has gotten himself into the lion's den. I think I closed my eyes out of pure shame for others. There are moments to recite poetry and there are moments to box. For me, that was one of the latter."

Friendship, as Bolaño shows it, corresponds to the dynamics between a diverse group in formation, but with the desire to belong, to be part: "For a moment I thought that Belano and Lima had forgotten about me, busy chatting with whatever extravagant character approached our table, but when it was starting to dawn they asked me if I wanted to belong to the gang. They didn't say 'group' or 'movement,' they said gang and I liked that. Of course, I said yes."

The behavior of friends changes with the arrival of women who are also part of the real visceralists, and with them romances, illusions, and disappointments, jealousy, and conflicts between friendships that become distant and reconcile, as happens in reality.

Bolaño called *The Savage Detectives* "a love letter to my generation" as testimony to what friendship means.

A. The Mentor/Guide

The archetype of the guide or mentor is easily recognizable in literature, and Virgil in Dante's *The Divine Comedy* exemplifies this role. As Dante's guide through Hell and Purgatory, Virgil leads him towards salvation, shielding him from the underworld's perils. He protects Dante, for example, by warning him not to look at the Gorgon, a gaze that would have eternally imprisoned him in Hell. Throughout Dante's journey, Virgil serves as a guide in both a physical and moral capacity, leading him through dangerous landscapes while also educating him about sin and divine justice.

Another important character is Gandalf a quintessential mentor figure in J.R.R. Tolkien's *The Hobbit* and *The Lord of the Rings*. Gandalf, a wizard belonging to the Istari order and the leader of the Company of the Ring, was named from the Old Norse "Catalogue of Dwarves." Gandalf's primary role is to lead, counsel, and unify the Free Peoples of Middle-earth in their resistance against Sauron. As a guide, he aids key characters in the novels on perilous journeys, offering both profound wisdom and practical expertise essential for navigating these quests. His teaching include the importance of trust, pity, and fellowship.

Charles Dickens is another important writer who often included characters who serve as wise counselors, offering guidance, moral clarity, or practical advice to protagonists facing adversity. As examples, in David Copperfield Betsey Trotwood is an eccentric great-aunt providing David with a home, support, and practical advice, helping to shape his character and future. Also, Mr. Micawber who offers David memorable advice on income and happiness: "Annual income twenty pounds, annual expenditure nineteen pounds nineteen shillings and sixpence, result happiness."

Dickens's wise counselors often share qualities such as empathy and understanding, a willingness to speak hard truths, and a life guided by principle and integrity. They provide practical support and encouragement, and possess the ability to inspire hope and resilience in those around them.

Another notable example is Mr. Brownlow in *Oliver Twist*, who acts as a benefactor and mentor to Oliver, offering him kindness, education, and a path away from the criminal underworld. Mr. Brownlow provides a moral example demonstrating the positive effect of guidance and support on individuals navigating difficult circumstances.

Joe Gargery in *Great Expectations* embodies kindness, humility, and unwavering integrity, serving as Pip's moral compass through his patient, forgiving nature and simple wisdom, grounding him amidst ambition and pride. In contrast, Miss Havisham, another character in this classic Dickens work, is a wealthy and eccentric unmarried woman who, after being abandoned at the altar, is consumed by bitterness. She manipulates and uses Pip, who is helped by Joe Gargery, his brother-in-law, a constant source of guidance for Pip, supporting him emotionally throughout the story.

B. The Solitary

An example of what solitude implies is found in Fyodor Dostoevsky's famous work *Crime and Punishment*, published in 1886. The behavior of the central character, Rodion Raskolnikov, before and after murdering an elderly moneylender, is frantic, pressured, and often frightened in his responses to the people he comes into contact with.

The loneliness and moral dilemma in which the malnourished and poor student finds himself in rich St. Petersburg torment him with confusion, paranoia, disgust, and bad conscience, feelings he cannot share.

Raskolnikov's problems and personality have been the subject of study and evaluation from a psychoanalytic point of view, especially the origins of that type of loneliness that manifests itself from the early years of life, particularly separation anxiety, personal or parental divorce, as well as the dilemma of the need that some feel to be alone and the incompatibility of loneliness with society, situations that are presented with great realism in Dostoevsky's work. Likewise, in the psychoanalytic field is found Erich Fromm's work *The Fear of Freedom* (also published as *Escape from Freedom*), in which he analyzes the fears that some people have of individual freedom, which causes them anxiety and alienation, and therefore they seek relief by renouncing freedom. Fromm differentiates between "freedom from," the liberation from external constraints, and "freedom to," the capacity to fulfill one's potential. While escaping external authority is crucial, the absence of positive freedom leaves individuals susceptible to the anxiety described by Dostoevsky's characters.

It can hardly be said that Rainer Maria Rilke was a solitary man, since in addition to having been married to sculptor Clara Westhoff and being a father, his life is full of torrid romances with rich and famous women, highlighting the writer and psychoanalyst Lou Andreas-Salomé. His life was a continuous journey from one temporary home to another, mainly in Italy, France, Germany, Scandinavia, North Africa, and Spain.

Despite the travels and affective adventures, the loneliness he experienced in Paris, which he details in great detail in a letter to Lou, represented a low point where the fear within him had grown rapidly. It was a city where people were simply 'transitory among passersby, abandoned and abandoned to themselves in their own destiny.'"

The Notebooks of Malte Laurids Brigge, a novel-diary, presents Rilke's vision of Paris. The narrator allows us to appreciate the profound loneliness he feels when walking through Paris or sitting on park benches from where he observes people with whom he finds no affinity, deepening his feeling of isolation. In *The Notebooks,* details are noted of the people passing by his side: "men and women, who are in some kind of transition, perhaps from madness to health, or perhaps to madness; all with something infinitely delicate in their faces, a love or knowledge or joy, as if it were a light that burns slowly, that surely could shine once more if only someone saw and helped . . ." "But there is no one to help."

Detailing the loneliness that the street produces in Malte, he writes in his notebook, "I often had to tell myself aloud that I was not one of them, that I would leave again that terrible city where they would die."

Although some critics think the novel is full of autobiographical details, it is important to keep in mind the ambiguity that Rilke faces, since he maintained a close relationship in Paris with the famous French sculptor Auguste Rodin in 1902, three years before writing *The Notebooks*. As Rodin's biographer and critic and later as his personal secretary, the relationship with the artist and his circle was relatively close. Moreover, possibly in the conversations with Rodin, one can trace the theories about art and the artist that are recorded in *Letters to a Young Poet*, Rilke's famous collection of advice to Franz Xaver Kappus.

Another way of presenting the solitary or solitude is found in the famous novel by the celebrated writer and philosopher Albert Camus, *The Fall*, which from the first sentence of the novel presents a monologue in the "first person" perspective, where the "I" and the "you" are used by a single person in a dynamic and intriguing narration.

"May I, sir, offer my services without running the risk of intruding?" asks the main character, Jean-Baptiste Clamence, a solitary judge who resides in Amsterdam, who with the excuse of helping a foreigner in a bar to order drinks initiates a conversation about the bartender's bad temper and the city. "Are you staying long in Amsterdam? A beautiful city, isn't it? Fascinating?" The dialogue continues, but the reader only hears the narrator and imagines what the other unknown character responds.

"Are you already leaving? Forgive me for having detained you. No, I beg you; I won't let you pay." In this way, a relationship has been established between two people, as the judge responds: "I will certainly be here tomorrow, as every night, and I will be delighted to accept your invitation."

The two characters will meet again, and a conversation will continue with Clamence's voice revealing his background, his personal existential problems, including a past experience that changed his life, which allows us to discover how solitary, empty, and absurd his life was.

Albert Camus, winner of the 1957 Nobel Prize in Literature, is one of the most influential French existentialist writers who has managed to apply literary talent to philosophy. In many of his works, like *The Fall* and *The Stranger,* it is possible to discover a nostalgic solitude. Camus was not afraid to isolate himself by opposing popular ideas at the time, which led him to break with Sartre and other powerful intellectuals in the 1950s who dominated the cultural scene in France. Unfortunately, Camus died relatively young in a tragic automobile accident in 1960.

He sought solitude in the belief that a personal experience could be a persuasive reference for literary and philosophical writing; that is reflected in his works.

Regarding contemporary authors, the characters in the novels of Michel Houellebecq, the famous and controversial French author born in Algeria, are people who generally have an unstable and solitary life, with short-term romantic interludes, generally unsatisfied. The repeated description of this type of character and their relationships in his novels, including *Submission*, follow a regular pattern, starting in student life, of which he tells us about school or university friends, who "disappear when we enter the workforce, plunging most of us into a solitude as stupefied as it is radical."

The novel was published in 2015, but the story ends in 2022 with the election of a Muslim as president of France. Due to its political and religious overtones, it turned out to be controversial and condemned by a large number of critics. Notwithstanding this aspect, in general, the novel concentrates on the dissipated lifestyle of the central character, and his conduct allows us to know solitude from another perspective.

The narrator is a cynical womanizer on the border of the pathological, as the author describes him. He is a professor who recognizes that he never had a vocation to practice a profession that he performs listlessly for many years out of inertia. Reflecting on his life empty of content, he recognizes that he had no qualms about sleeping with his students, and the age difference didn't matter to him. His contempt for women is explicit when he presents Aurélie as one of his passing adventures, and thinks with a certain contempt that she would soon "give up any matrimonial ambition, her imperfectly extinguished sensuality would lead her to seek the company of young men, she would become what we used to call a cougar, and would undoubtedly continue on this path for several years, ten at most, before the drowning of her flesh became prohibitive, and condemned her to lasting solitude." The same fate awaits Sandra, another adventure that confirms the narrator's solitude, who is incapable of establishing lasting relationships and feeling remorse or empathy.

Solitude is considered by some therapists as the worst disease of our century, as millions of people in the richest countries are victims of depression, alcoholism, and drugs as palliatives.

The symptoms are palpable on social media networks and dating websites that replace classified ad pages, showing dozens of people in search of companionship.

C. The Exile/Outsider

Exile operates on multiple levels: geographical, social, psychological, and spiritual, which is particularly evident in our hyper-connected social media landscape, as many individuals grapple with loneliness and alienation, even within the confines of their own homes or countries.

To comprehend the essence of exile or the definition of an outsider, Odysseus emerges as a multifaceted character, embodying both the roles of exile and outsider throughout *The Odyssey* and its associated Greek myths. Throughout much of the epic, Odysseus experiences exile, both physically and existentially. For a decade after the Trojan War, he is prevented from returning to Ithaca, forced to wander the seas and confront various challenges. This separation from his homeland also represents a deeper isolation, as he is distanced from his roles as king, husband, and father, thus losing his sense of identity.

Throughout his travels, Odysseus is consistently portrayed as an outsider, a stranger reliant on the benevolence of others. He frequently employs disguises and assumes various personas to guarantee his survival and accomplish his objectives. Even upon his return to Ithaca, he remains in disguise as a beggar, concealing his true identity until he reveals himself to Telemachus, his son, and together they plan how to deal with the suitors. This outsider status is not merely circumstantial; it is an integral aspect of his character, compelling him to constantly adapt and perform, preventing him from being his authentic self until he reclaims his rightful place.

Another example of this character archetype is Meursault, the protagonist of Albert Camus's *The Stranger*, who is widely regarded as an outsider due to his emotional detachment, unconventional behavior, and inability—or refusal—to conform to societal expectations. His lack of grief at his mother's funeral, his indifference to relationships, and his moral nihilism set him apart from those around him. Society perceives him as cold, amoral, and even monstrous, particularly because he does not display the expected emotions at his mother's death and later, at his trial, he is judged more for this lack of feeling than for the crime he commits.

Exile in James Joyce's play *Exiles* is presented both literally and figuratively. On a literal level, Richard Rowan and Bertha, two main characters, have physically returned to Dublin after nine years abroad, echoing Joyce's own self-imposed exile from Ireland. However, their return does not resolve their sense of displacement; instead, it highlights a deeper spiritual and emotional estrangement. The play's title itself, if read as multifaceted "exiles" of each single person, signals that exile is not just about geography, but about the alienation individuals experience from each other, from society, and even from themselves. This multifaceted exile permeates the characters' interactions and inner lives, thereby shaping their identities and destinies within the narrative.

Joyce's literary sensibilities were profoundly influenced by the works of Henrik Ibsen, as evident in *Exiles*, which emulate Ibsen's *When We Dead Awaken*. This play mirrors the complexities relationships, disillusionment, expectations, and yearning for artistic and personal freedom experienced by its character archetypes.

Charlotte Brontë's *Jane Eyre* protagonist experiences profound physical and social isolation from a tender age. As an orphan, she resides with her aunt, Mrs. Reed, who fails to provide her with the nurturing and acceptance she craves. Despite residing in their household, Jane is emotionally and socially marginalized, effectively becoming an outsider within her own family. Throughout the novel, her outsider status, whether as an orphan, a poor relation, or a governess, prevents her from achieving a sense of belonging within any social group.

Henry David Thoreau's sojourn at Walden Pond is frequently characterized as a form of self-imposed seclusion. However, this "exile" did not entail a complete withdrawal from societal engagement. Instead, it constituted a purposeful endeavor to live in simplicity and intentionality, a pursuit of personal development and moral clarity. Thoreau himself penned:

> I went to the woods because I wished to live deliberately, to front only the essential facts of life, and see if I could not learn what it had to teach, and not, when I came to die, discover that I had not lived.

Thoreau's "exile" described in his famous book *Walden; or, Life in the Woods* was metaphorical as well as physical. He sought solitude to examine life's essentials, free from society's distractions and conventions, but remained connected to the world. His cabin was near Concord, Massachusetts, and he entertained visitors and engaged with social and political issues like abolition and civil disobedience.

Epilogue

Human nature is complex, and the typology of personalities encompasses numerous profiles and situations as described here, which represent only a very small and arbitrarily selected sample of the universe of characteristics and characters that are described in the works of Theophrastus, Jean de La Bruyère, and Álvaro Uribe that inspire this essay.

I have been fortunate read the works referenced in this essay, and have been particularly excited to learn about human nature and characters while reading them. Books have been important sources and conduits for understanding some aspects of the human soul. To conclude, I am fortunate to find in the latest column of Jesús Silva Herzog Márquez, dedicated to the most recent book by the founder of the Nexus Institute, Dutch essayist Rob Riemen, *The Art of Being Human*, a way to end this essay that I hope will serve as a stimulus to explore the cited works.

Only books (and other works of art) that show us like a mirror what we don't want to see, those that confront us with fundamental questions whose answers we don't have, those that remind us of the knowledge and wisdom we had forgotten, those that teach us to read the book of our own life and that, precisely by telling us the truth, encourage and console us: only these books help us return to ourselves, to our better self, to thus change the course of history.

—Jesús Silva Herzog Márquez.
Books, *Reforma*, November 4, 2023

A.I. Summary

This summary was written by *Claude,* an AI assistant developed by Anthropic.

This extensive non-academic essay explores human character archetypes through literary analysis, drawing inspiration from classical character studies by Theophrastus, Jean de la Bruyère, and contemporary author Álvaro Uribe.

The work examines universal human traits and behaviors by analyzing fictional characters from classic and contemporary novels, incorporating philosophical and psychological perspectives to illuminate the complexities of human nature.

Introduction

Establishes the framework for character analysis inspired by classical essayists and outlines the author's approach to examining human nature through literary characters. The author acknowledges the overlapping nature of character categories and potential analytical limitations.

I. Destructive Passions

Explores toxic relationships and harmful emotional patterns through psychoanalytic lenses (Freud, Jung, Fromm, Yalom), examining how destructive impulses manifest in human connections.

A. The Obsessed

Analyzes characters driven by singular pursuits that lead to self-destruction, featuring

Don Quixote, Captain Ahab, Heathcliff, and Humbert Humbert as examples of how passion transforms into destructive obsession.

B. The Jealous, Envious and the Hater

Examines destructive emotions through Spinoza's philosophical framework and René Girard's mimetic theory, using Shakespeare's Othello and Dostoevsky's works to illustrate how envy leads to scapegoating.

C. Seducer/Seduced

Investigates seduction dynamics through literary figures like Don Juan, Casanova, and characters from novels by Benjamin Constant, Tolstoy, and Stendhal, exploring power imbalances in romantic relationships.

D. The Innocent/Naif

Studies characters marked by vulnerability and lack of worldly experience, primarily through Voltaire's Candide and Dostoevsky's Prince Myshkin.

II. Travelers and Walkers

Celebrates the tradition of literary wanderers and the significance of movement in human experience, featuring Thomas Hardy's countryside descriptions and various travel narratives.

III. The Diplomats

Examines diplomatic character traits beyond official roles, drawing from Machiavelli's "The Prince" and various historical and literary examples of negotiation and statecraft.

IV. Those Who Face Death
Confronts mortality through philosophical perspectives (Camus, Husserl, Derrida) and literary works by Tolstoy, Mann, and others who grapple with death's inevitability.

V. The Terrorist
Analyzes extremist characters through Joseph Conrad's prophetic novels "The Secret Agent" and "Under Western Eyes," examining the psychology of political violence.

VI. Wealth, Influence, and Fame
Critiques materialism and social climbing through works by Trollope, Fitzgerald, and Shakespeare, incorporating philosophical perspectives from Montaigne, Schopenhauer, and Nietzsche.

VII. Friends
Explores authentic friendship through letter collections and novels, contrasting genuine connection with superficial social networking.

A. The Mentor/Guide
Examines guiding figures in literature, from Virgil in Dante's "Divine Comedy" to Dickens' wise counselors.

B. The Solitary
Studies isolation through Dostoevsky's "Crime

and Punishment," Rilke's "Notebooks," Camus' "The Fall," and contemporary works.

C. The Exile/Outsider
Investigates displacement and alienation through characters like Odysseus, Meursault from "The Stranger," and Joyce's "Exiles."

Quoted Sources and Their Contributions
The essay integrates diverse philosophical, psychological, and literary sources to support its character analysis:

A. Philosophical Foundations
Hannah Arendt and Jean-Paul Sartre provide existential frameworks for understanding the human condition and freedom.

Baruch Spinoza's "Ethics" offers systematic categorization of human emotions, particularly jealousy and envy.

Arthur Schopenhauer contributes perspectives on human needs, suffering, and life stages.

Albert Camus, Edmund Husserl, and Jacques Derrida provide varied approaches to confronting mortality.

B. Psychological Perspectives
Sigmund Freud's concepts of death drive and repetition compulsion illuminate destructive relationships.

Carl Jung's theories of projection and shadow explain relationship dynamics.

Erich Fromm and Irvin Yalom contribute existential therapeutic insights.

René Girard's mimetic theory explains scapegoating and social violence.

C. Literary Sources

The essay draws extensively from canonical works, with Russian literature (Tolstoy, Dostoevsky, Chekhov) providing psychological depth, French literature (Constant, Stendhal, Camus) offering sophisticated character analysis, and English literature (Shakespeare, Dickens, Hardy) supplying archetypal figures. Contemporary works bridge classical insights with modern concerns.

D. Historical and Political Analysis

Niccolò Machiavelli informs understanding of diplomatic and political characters.

Henry Kissinger and Francis Fukuyama provide modern perspectives on terrorism and statecraft.

Historical correspondence (Churchill, Mann, Hesse) offers authentic insights into human relationships.

Strengths and Weaknesses

The essay's ambitious scope demonstrates how literary characters serve as vehicles for understanding universal human traits. The integration of multiple disciplinary perspectives creates a rich analytical framework that avoids reductive categorization.

The author acknowledges several weaknesses:

the arbitrary nature of character categories, potential oversimplification of complex personalities, and occasional questionable interpretations. The non-academic format, while accessible, sometimes lacks analytical rigor.

The work connects classical literary insights with modern concerns, particularly in discussions of terrorism, social media isolation, and contemporary relationship dynamics.

Conclusion

"Profiles, Situations, Characters" is an exploratory essay that uses literature as a lens for examining human nature. While lacking scholarly rigor, it demonstrates how fictional characters can illuminate real psychological and social patterns. The work's strength lies in its comprehensive survey of literary archetypes and its integration of diverse intellectual traditions, making it valuable for readers seeking to understand the enduring relevance of classic literature to human experience.

Note: The previous section (pages 101–106) was written by Claude, an AI assistant developed by Anthropic, based on specific instructions and content provided by the author. The author supplied the framework, sources, themes, and direction for the text, while Claude generated the written analysis following those guidelines. The introduction was then lightly edited by a proofreader for clarity and consistent tone. This collaborative approach reflects the author's intent to utilize AI capabilities for drafting portions of the analytical work, with the human author retaining responsibility for the conceptual design, source selection, and overall direction of the essay. This disclosure is provided for transparency regarding the methods used in producing the front matter of this book.

www.ingramcontent.com/pod-product-compliance
Lightning Source LLC
Chambersburg PA
CBHW030552130626
46552CB00006B/2518